Dedication

With love to Miss Bea,

Joyce, Mil, Viola,

and Irene

Healing Design

Practical Feng Shui for Healthy and Gracious Living

Hope Karan Gerecht

Journey Editions

Boston · Tokyo

Acknowledgments

Respect and thanks to my family for their love. An immense hug to my friends in Baltimore—my Baltimore buddies.

To Claire Gerus, my friend and agent, thank you on so many levels—not only for the title of the book, but also for finding the perfect home for Healing Design.

Deepest gratitude to my teachers, both in person and through their writings. I especially thank Cheiro, for your intuition and understanding of color, and professor Thomas Lin Yun for your humble reverence, humor, and rich wisdom.

Grateful thanks also to Linda Montgomery and Linda Joy Burke for your wonderful, artistic interpretations of the nature of the five elements, and to photographers Jan Nathan Boreli, Peter Butler, James Chen, Mark Dolce, Catherine Glayvia, and Ron Kraus. For their beautiful visual and textual designs, my gratitude to Peter Blaiwas and Brian Hotchkiss at Vernon Press. For their typing support, my appreciation to Sherri Bearman, Charlotte Walters, Sallie Levitt, and Patricia McCarty. Editing thanks to Marie Salter. I also want to thank Cindy Ong for illustrations and Romulus Gilmore, Jerry McClellan, and Rennie Radoccia for floor plans and site plans.

My appreciation to Michael Kerber, Jan Johnson, P. J. Tierney, and Greg Brandenburgh at Charles E. Tuttle Publishing Co. for all of your efforts on behalf of Healing Design. Many thanks to each of the owners of the projects that appear in this book.

To Jessica Dibb, Bob Brown, and Karen McKuen for your help in keeping the energy moving. To Ron Kraus for your love, wisdom, and wry humor. And to Jeannie Dalmas, my friend of thirty years, the woman I honor as the midwife of this book—for your unconditional time and support were truly pure grace.

First published in 1999 by Journey Editions, an imprint of Periplus Editions (HK) Ltd., with offices at 153 Milk Street, Boston, Massachusetts 02109 and Tuttle Building, 1-2-6, Suido, Bunkyo-Ku, Tokyo 112, Japan

Copyright ©1999 Hope Gerecht

Library of Congress Cataloging-in-Publication Data

Gerecht, Hope Karan,
Healing Design : Practical Feng Shui for Healthy and Gracious Living / Hope Karen Gerecht.
     p.   cm.
ISBN-1-885203-60-8
1. Feng-shui.   I. Title.
6F1779.F4G47   1999
133.3'337—dc21   99-19468
                                             CIP

Distributed by

USA
Tuttle Publishing
Distribution Center
Airport Industrial Park
364 Innovation Drive
Tel.: (802) 773-8930
    (800) 526-2778
Fax.: (802) 773-6993

Japan
Tuttle Shokai Inc.
1-21-13, Seki
Tama-ku, Kawasaki-shi
Kanagawa-ken, 214, Japan
Tel.: (044) 833-0225
Fax.: (044) 822-0413

Southeast Asia
Berkeley Books, Pte. Ltd.
5 Little Road #08-01
Singapore 536983
Tel.: (65) 280-3320
Fax.: (64) 280-6290

Credits and acknowledgments: Every effort has been made to obtain appropriate permissions and to credit copyright holders. Rights holders who wish to contact the publisher should communicate with the Editorial offices of Tuttle Publishing, 153 Milk Street, Boston, Massachusetts 02109.

Text and cover design by Peter M. Blaiwas, Vernon Press, Inc.
Five element illustrations ©1999 Linda Montgomery
Bagua diagram illustrations courtesy of Cindy Ong
Photo credits(unless listed below, photographs by Hope Karan Gerecht.)
Jan Nathan Borell, Berkeley Springs, West Virginia: p. 20; James Chen, Santa Barbara California: pp. 96,99,101,104 and 107; Mark A. Dolce, Jerome, Arizona: pp. 44, 50, 53, 54, and 58(right); Catherine Giayvia, Baltimore, Maryland: pp. 8, 84,86, 88, 90, n93, 94, 112, 113, and 115; Ron Kraus, Bal;timore, Maryland: from jacket and pp., 46, 56, 58(left), 60, 62, 64, 66(bottom), 69, 70, and 128; Sharon Lampron, Baltimore, Maryland: pp. 41(bottom), 42(left), 72, 76, 78, and 81
Site and floor plan credits:
Architecture Works, Clarkdale, Arizona: p. 48; Romulus Gilmore, Baltimore, Maryland: pp. 89,98,110,121, and 133; Jerry McClellan: p. 6

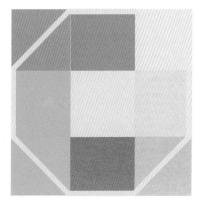

Contents

Preface

Feng shui—what a concept! The idea that the items in our homes and the way they are arranged can affect our lives might seem unbelievable. Yet here it is, alive, strong, and in use for thousands of years. It is the energy and soul of both interior and exterior design.

The beginnings of feng shui date back somewhere between four thousand and six thousand years. Exactitude in dating only becomes easier for more recent history, but we do know that one thousand years ago more than one hundred twenty schools of feng shui existed. China's vastness and its multitude of provinces, each with its own feng shui master, led to some conflicting theories and many shared truths.

The various schools of feng shui all hold three main tenets: (1) to elevate our life by encouraging the flow of vital energy (*chi*) in our living environments; (2) to deflect unfortunate energy (*sha*); and (3) to create balance in our home through reference to the five aspects of nature: Water, Wood, Fire, Earth, and Metal. As increased, balanced chi meanders gently through our home and workplace, we may experience better health, enhanced creativity and happiness, a deeper wisdom and spiritual connection, more rewarding relationships, stronger career support, and increased prosperity.

Feng shui encompasses decorating on a whole new level—with intention. Instead of focusing simply on style and function, which are certainly important, feng shui takes into account the way the shapes, colors, and materials you choose affect you and others in your home. *Healing Design* will provide many ideas on everything from small touches to dramatic ways to enhance your living and working environments. You may choose to make sweeping changes in your home, but generally this is not necessary. Often small changes are sufficient to raise and balance the beneficial chi of the specific symbolic areas in your home.

I found writing this book to be a unique challenge. It caused me to grapple with just how to convey something as subtle as energy, an invisible commodity, by using a language that has little history of doing this, and that certainly has few applicable terms. The eight sites visited in *Healing Design,* and their feng shui readings, are meant to demonstrate the subtle, exquisite energy behind form and matter.

Toward the end of my four years of studying interior design, I discovered my first book on feng shui. Finally, I thought, I've found a traditional system that provides the answers I've been seeking and includes the serendipitous benefits of rich symbolism and ritual, of which we are certainly bereft in this modern day and age.

Now, twelve years and more than eight hundred feng shui projects later, I am still in awe of the insight and process of feng shui. John Lennon and Paul McCartney's album and song title "Magical Mystery Tour" closely describes feng shui. It is a process that often seems magical as it leads you on a mysterious voyage into a deep and rich examination and understanding of your life.

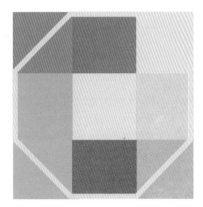

The Essence of Feng Shui

Chi is the nonbiological self—our spirit, our psyche, our essence.
—Professor Thomas Lin Yun, *Feng Shui Master*

Feng shui, literally "wind and water," is an ancient Chinese discipline used to design and decorate the home or workplace. The homes we visit in this book exemplify the magic balance and charm that feng shui brings to a space. Those who use feng shui believe it changes lives. Improved health, increased business and career advancement, support in creating closer relationships, increased spirituality, deepened wisdom, and ultimately feelings of greater joy and happiness can be yours with feng shui.

A New View: Chi

In our daily lives, energy surrounds and embraces us; it is the very essence of our being. We would all agree that our physical activities require some degree of energy or exertion—this is fairly obvious. What might not be so obvious to us, however, is the underlying energy of things and of dwellings, in particular.

Traditional cultures are sensitive to life's energetic matrix, describing it with their own terms such as *prana* in India, *qi* in Japan, *chi* in China, *ruach* in Hebrew, *lung* in Tibet, *pneuma* in Greece, and *ankh* in early Egypt. Not surprisingly, there are no comparable terms in the West, but we might translate chi as "vital life energy" or "breath of life."

Human chi can be thought of as an electromagnetic skeleton for the body, an unseen supportive framework created by circuits of electrical energy. Practitioners of tai-chi ch'uan and other martial arts may develop chi to such an extent that they can perform incredible physical feats. A few very advanced martial artists have been able to direct a forceful stream of energy out of their upward-turned hands, sending an opponent flying across the room without physically touching him. Karate masters martial their chi before hand-chopping through stacks of bricks or thick wooden boards.

Right
The person who sits in the chair can receive an uneasy feeling from the sharp point of this table as it angles toward the desk.

There are many types of chi: Heaven chi is seen in weather and astronomy while earth chi gives rise to mountains, lush vegetation, and flowing water. Animal chi differentiates among the characteristics of species and human chi is present in the health and energy patterns of a person. Dwelling chi determines the specific energy of a building. Feng shui looks at the interrelationship of all these facets of chi, but examines dwelling chi especially, taking into account the shapes, compass orientations, colors, furnishings, and building materials of a site.

Simple rearrangement of furniture; careful placement of plants, lights, mirrors, and other decorative items; and conscious use of color can affect us deeply.

When practicing feng shui, thousands of principles can come into play to create healthy and harmonious living spaces. A subtle, pleasant sense of comfort and ease is often experienced in areas where this art has been applied. Feng shui adjustments are "site specific." Requirements needed to balance one environment may be completely different for another.

Raising and balancing the beneficial chi of an area with some of the feng shui methods shown in *Healing Design* will help you attain your goals in many areas of your life: health, spirituality, relationships, creativity, knowledge, and career.

In addition to creating healthy and harmonious living and working environments, feng shui facilitates increased luck—fortunate actions drawn into your life—and success. The Chinese believe that we are born with luck that is either good, average, or unfortunate. It is generally obvious when a person was born with poor luck. Try as they might, life seldom treats them well. The difference between being born with average or good luck is more subtle, but good luck manifests in a high level of synchronicity and, when difficult situations occur, someone with good luck invariably comes out on top. If a person born with average luck does feng shui, the Chinese believe that person will be luckier than one born with good luck who does not practice feng shui.

How Does It Work?

Feng shui encourages fine attention to the details of design and to the movement of energy. For more than three thousand years, masters, teachers, and practitioners of feng shui have chronicled the effects of various aspects of living environments on people's lives. This has resulted in the documentation of thousands of principles that constitute the various schools of feng shui.

Feng shui is both an art and a science. The scientific, or masculine, side is the *yang* facet of feng shui. By using geography, astronomy, the compass, and mathematical calculations, one is able to best position oneself, according to feng shui principles, for maximum comfort and prosperity. Another important aspect of the art of feng shui is *yin*, or the feminine, intuitive side. After understanding and working with the concise rules of feng shui, spend a few moments of quiet, meditative time in each area of your home, getting a feeling for what flows and what doesn't flow, what inspires and what doesn't, what you find beautiful and what might need enhancing.

Once a person is "well positioned" according to feng shui principles, changes and enhancements are made using an assortment of interchangeable "cures," or symbolic beautiful items. There are also a number of colors—hues, tints, and tones—from which one can choose to balance the elements or raise the chi of a residence to a higher degree.

What Does It Mean?

The Chi of Heaven, Earth, and Humans

"Kan yu," an ancient term for feng shui, means "Raise the head and observe the sky above; lower the head and observe the environment around us." A graphic portrayal of this philosophy is seen in ikebana, the Japanese art of flower arranging, which emphasizes form and balance. Here, the upper branch of the traditional arrangement represents heaven, the lower branch earth, and the line in between humans—the balance point between and the blending of heaven and earth. The goal of feng shui is to bring harmony and balance among the influx of heaven and earth energies and their influences on human lives.

Many Levels of Support

An early translation of feng shui was "to cover and support." Ideally, this is what our living environments at home and work should do: They should cover or protect us and provide support emotionally, physically, mentally, and spiritually.

Emotional support from our environment helps us to feel comfortable and at ease, providing a general feeling of safety when we are at work or play, or just relaxing. *Physical support* assists our bodies ergonomically. Supportive, well-proportioned designs in furnishings and ample space in which to move through rooms gracefully bring ease and comfort. *Mental support* stimulates our minds. Interesting items in our living spaces and subtle changes to our environments help us keep a fresh perspective and remind us that change is the only constant in the universe.

We thrive on change and, at the same time, often fear it. We may find comfort in familiar objects, but this may lead to clutter, which diminishes mental support. Piles of unmoving papers, or a collection of anything that doesn't change much, can weigh heavily on our minds. Creating order in our living environments by getting rid of any excess (books overflowing from stuffed bookcases, for example, or stacks of old papers and magazines lying about) makes room for learning and moving forward with lucid thoughts and inspirations; it clears a path for positive change.

Plants and devotional objects contribute to making this windowsill into a sacred space.

Spiritual support comes from beauty in our living environments. In his book *Care of the Soul*, Thomas Moore observes, "The soul is nurtured by beauty. What food is to the body, arresting, complex, and pleasing images are to the soul." Our surroundings should be nurturing: filled with colors and objects that especially delight and inspire us.

Living Energy

The most current translation of feng shui, "wind and water," is the best way to understand and experience the chi energy moving on the earth and in our environments. When there is too much wind, we have a hurricane or a tornado; too much water, a flood or erosion. When there is no wind, a hot August day

The Five Elements

In Chinese cosmology, in addition to yin/yang, the process of change is understood through a system called Five Element Theory. Yin/yang and Five Element Theory are the basis for the discipline of acupuncture, feng shui, all of the Eastern arts, science, medicine, and philosophy. Also referred to as "the five changes," "the five phases," or "the five moving agents," the five elements—water, wood, fire, earth, and metal—are an intimate way to connect with and understand nature. These elements are metaphors for the different forms and qualities of energy.

The constant movement of chi energy can be seen as we follow the two cycles of change—the nourishing cycle and the control cycle— through the five elements. We'll examine the nourishing cycle first. Depicted in the outer circle of the illustration, it shows how one element creates, nourishes, and supports the next element in this generative sequence.

The Nourishing Cycle
Water–Wood–Fire–Earth–Metal

As part of the supportive, nourishing cycle, water evaporates and rains down to nourish the wood element: trees, grass, flowers, and all vegetation. We cut down trees for the wood to create and feed fires. Fire is the molten mass of energy at the center of the earth. When the earth expels this molten energy, it reduces matter to ash, creating even more earth. Earth produces minerals that combine to

becomes stifling and uncomfortable, and with too little water, a garden struggles to grow. We thrive when conditions are balanced somewhere in the middle. Gentle breezes and meandering streams are pleasant, refreshing, and have a beneficial effect on us. So it is with feng shui: The ideal is to have a median, balanced flow of chi in our living environments.

Just as houseplants require their own specific mixes of the elements—water, air, light, nutrients—humans have many basic elemental needs. We spend much of our lives trying to satisfy these needs, even though we may not know precisely what we seek. According to Richard Heinberg, editor and publisher of the journal *MuseLetter*, today our basic needs are speaking more loudly than ever as a result of increased time spent indoors—in homes, workplaces, malls, and cars—

create metal. Minerals from the metal element form our mineral water, and the cycle continues.

The Control Cycle
Water–Fire–Metal–Wood–Earth

The control cycle is nature's built-in check-and-balance system, and helps keep energy from running rampantly out of balance. The restraining control cycle (the inner star pattern in the previous illustration) is best illuminated with water extinguishing fire. Likewise, fire melts metal, as in blacksmithing. Metal implements, such as axes, can be used to cut down trees (wood). Tree roots break up the earth, and earth absorbs water and also creates boundaries for ponds and rivers.

These models of energetic movement and the patterns they manifest can be found in every area of life, from our psychological states of mind to the health of our bodies; from the spheres of the heavenly bodies to the contours, shapes, colors, and compass directions of the earth. Everything in the universe can be organized to correspond with the Five Element Theory and, in turn, this theory can help us to better understand the world and our place in it. (To acquaint you with this elemental world, many examples of the elements are shown in the homes visited. To further increase your understanding, see the wonderful Five Element artwork and poetry in chapter 2. In chapter 11, you will find charts to calculate your personal elemental make-up, as well as in-depth descriptions covering the five elements.)

lessening the soul's nourishment, which is available in the subtle currents of life force flowing in nature. Although we may not know it, we are deeply affected by the chi, or energetic matrices, of our surroundings.

In this book, you will learn how to balance your home environment by beginning to identify yin/yang, the five elements, and what your needs are in relation to these energetic influences. This is quite a different and unique way to look at the design of your home. In addition to style and function, feng shui focuses on the impact of shapes, colors, and materials on your home and workplace. Quite often, small changes are sufficient to adjust the feng shui energetic movement of a room.

The Tao of Design

Feng shui can be described as the tao, or the way, of design. In Chinese philosophy, *tao* means unity and is symbolized by the outer circle encompassing the two halves of the yin/yang symbol. The outer circle symbolizes wholeness. Inside the circle, the yin (dark half) and the yang (light half) graphically depict a flattened two-dimensional representation of the spiral of DNA, the basic building block of life. All of life is contained within the tao and is constantly changing. The yin night moves into the yang day. Yin winter changes to spring (a more equal mix of yin/yang) and then to yang summer. While all things predominantly manifest either yin or yang, they always contain some proportion of both. On a hot, yang summer day, cool yin shadows are found under the trees. In the dark evening yin sky, there are bright, sparkling yang stars. (For a more detailed discussion of yin/yang, see chapter 11.)

All life is in motion within the cycles of nature. Change and transformation, when kept in balance between the polarities of yin/yang, lead to harmony. With the goals of maintaining balance and unity, the focus of feng shui may begin from the inside out so that you gain a clearer understanding of what you wish to create in your life. Or you may contemplate the events in your outer life, looking for clues to which areas require increased harmony. The tao sees no separation between our inner experience and the external world; it addresses the experience of simply being with the wholeness of life. Feng shui is a path of exploring the wholeness of life—a moving meditation with your life at the center of the wheel.

In nature, one rarely sees the straight lines found in modern architecture.

Theories

The various schools of feng shui are sometimes in basic disagreement with each other because they have developed in different areas of China, as well as in other countries, and so reflect regional beliefs and customs. One school is more technical and finds the others to be too folkloric. Another believes the other schools are too dogmatic and out of touch with modern times. Still another feels that its teachings are most faithful to the traditional teachings. Some use the compass, others don't. Despite these disparities, value can be found in each school.

To some extent, *Healing Design* is a melding of various schools of feng shui. I have endeavored to bring together the most important, universal truths from these schools to assist you in creating your own healing, supportive environments. Occasionally, you may find conflicting information from the different schools, particularly concerning the use of color. Use feng shui as your guide. After you study the options presented, turn them over to your intuitive side, which will help you make the most appropriate choices. Always seek balance between heaven chi, earth chi, and human chi.

Getting Started

Now, from a feng shui perspective, prepare to look around your surroundings, exploring your living space in a new way. You may want to read chapter 11 to determine your personal feng shui so you will have an internal reference point as you begin to apply these teachings to your home and workplace.

When discussing feng shui, I immediately share three basic, and probably the most important, general rules: (1) have nothing broken in your home, (2) get rid of clutter, and (3) rid yourself of things you do not love.

Broken Items

The negative chi of a broken item brings the energy of everything around it down. Broken window panes, which represent the eyes or the way we see things, cracked glass in picture frames, corners chipped off mirrors, electronic equipment in need of repair, and many other items constantly remind us of their faults and inadequacies, thereby producing negative chi. Therefore, anything that is broken should be discarded, unless it can be repaired in a complete way. For example, if you have a table and one of the legs comes out, it is fine to glue or fasten the leg back in place. If the leg were to break in two, however, it would not be a complete repair simply to glue the two halves back together. The broken chi, or disrupted energy field, would always have an effect on anything near the table, including you. You could have a new leg made by a craftsperson, which would restore positive chi, or you could discard the table, which would remove the broken chi from your life.

Set aside a little time, perhaps forty-five minutes, to look at the feng shui in your home. Start at the front door, notepad in hand, and work your way from room to room, recording changes that must be made to anything that is broken or doesn't work as well as it could. Are any doors difficult to open? (This may signify struggle in your life.) When you open your front door, does it remain open? Doors are the primary path by which chi enters our homes. If they constantly swing closed of their own accord, the entrance and circulation of chi are hampered, which symbolizes limited opportunities. Do windows open easily and stay in place once opened? Are all of the glass panes in your home's windows clear and unbroken? Are your appliances, lamps, and electronic equipment in good working order? Now is the time to repair or discard any nonworking items. Although we may tell ourselves that we will fix things "sometime soon," time has a way of eluding us, and repair plans set for one weekend may still be waiting years later. Ridding yourself of broken items will raise the level of smooth and healthy chi in your home.

Clear Clutter

All the feng shui adjustments in the world cannot override the impeding effects of clutter, which detracts from harmony and movement in a space. Clearing the clutter is the symbolic equivalent to clearing the mind through meditation.

Seek Beauty

The third step is to begin to rid yourself of things you do not love. Your surroundings are an important part of your life. When you consciously change the enjoyment level of items in your home and office from just okay to pleasing, you tell yourself that you are no longer "settling" for a lower quality of life. This positive change in thought has subtle yet profound effects on your life: You may attract positive, interesting situations into your life more easily, and you will undoubtedly experience improvement in your general feelings of happiness and peace.

When beginning this process, some people feel they have too many items to replace and don't know where to start. Often, we may have emotional attachments to items we no longer like, or we may hold on to items that we never really liked because we are still able to use them. We may have purchased furniture or decorative objects many years ago but not updated them to suit our changing tastes. All of these things should be reviewed carefully.

Consider Ann's story: Ann and her husband bought their home almost two years ago, and, even though much work has been done, she says it doesn't "feel" like her home. Not coincidentally, in the past few years Ann's parents have been replacing some of their furniture, sending their old furniture to Ann. These pieces fill the rooms in Ann's home more out of sentiment than for her enjoyment. The art studio she has been trying to create sits idle, furnished with her parent's things, which do not particularly interest her. The studio is ready to use, but there is no spark, no inspiration drawing Ann into the room in which she intends to explore her creativity.

We form connections to our surroundings and the items in it. Even though we may not think we spend much time looking at the rooms in our homes, our surroundings deeply affect us on both conscious and subconscious levels.

Zen Surfaces

Keep walls, counters, desks, and tables at least 50 percent clear to strike a balance between what stimulates your attention and what allows your mind to rest.

This is a good time, at the beginning of the process, to take your notepad and do another forty-five minute walk-through of your home with a new feng shui purpose. This time, instead of settling for furniture or items that are just okay, make a list of everything you do not absolutely love. Know that eventually you would like to replace these with items you consider to be great. This plan may take some time to carry out, but you'll be surprised at the profound effects even small changes can create. Are there items that would be more pleasing to you with a coat of paint? Might a piece of furniture be slipcovered for renewed beauty? Are some rooms overcrowded, in need of selective "weeding"? Take stock of what does and does not excite you about every room in your home. If you don't love something and it is small, remove it. Nature abhors a vacuum, and something will at some point appear to replace it, if it needs replacing.

Perhaps a pared-down, Zen-like approach to decorating will feel more calming. Create a list of items you wish to change and how they will change: painting, slipcovering, removing, or replacing. Now, prioritize. You may wish to start with easy changes, or you could start with changes you feel will have the strongest impact on your space. Whatever you decide, you will feel uplifted the moment the plan you choose is put into action. You may want to swap some time with a friend who likes to paint. Get some ideas from how-to books on furniture painting techniques, or hire an experienced craftsperson. Create a budget for replacing some of the larger items you no longer love, and keep your eyes open for replacement possibilities.

Feng shui is a perpetual ongoing process, a lifestyle, in fact. Begin now to discover the wonder and peace it brings.

Feng Shui Principles

My house here is painted the yellow color of fresh butter on the outside with glaringly green shutters. It is completely whitewashed inside, and the floor is made of red tiles. And over it there is the intensely blue sky. In this I can live and breathe, meditate, and paint.
—Vincent van Gogh, *Artist*

The Ba-gua

Feng shui is concerned with the eight most important areas of life and the numerous ways we can support ourselves in attaining our various life goals. These eight areas—family/health, wealth, helpful people/travel, children/creativity, wisdom/general knowledge, fame/advancement, career, and love—are laid out in an

Page 20
Near the centers of a traditional
American town square, it's not unusual to
find an octagonal gazebo.

Below and opposite
In some schools, the compass assigns
life areas; in others the positions of the
life areas depend upon the placement of
the entrance to the property or home.

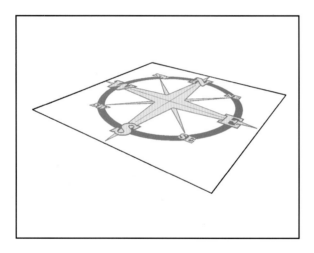

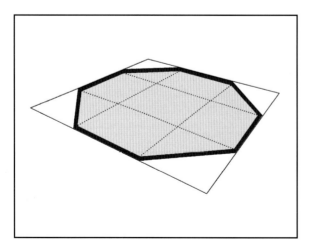

octagonal pattern called the *ba-gua* (phonetically, ba-kwa). The ba-gua, an ancient pattern, is based on the *I Ching,* a five-thousand-year-old system of philosophy and divination. It symbolizes the movement and connectedness of all aspects of life. The octagon, particularly when surrounded by the eight trigrams (sacred emblems made of linear patterns that represent yin/yang and the changing forces of the universe: heaven, earth, thunder, water, mountain, wind, fire, and lake) of the *I Ching*, is considered the luckiest shape in feng shui for attracting positive chi and repelling negativity.

The layout of the ba-gua, visually superimposed like a transparency and oriented to the entrance, derives from the popular school of feng shui called the Black Hat Sect of Tibetan Tantric Buddhism. In effect, different parts of your life are assigned to areas in the physical world: an extremely potent way to "ensoul" your environment. As you consciously place items you truly enjoy in certain areas, you clarify and focus intentions in your mind and create focal points in your living environment. Objects, colors, plants, and lighting then act as beautiful, pleasant reminders of what you are attempting to create in your life.

Feng shui consists of thousands of principles, yet, at the same time, offers an enormous amount of flexibility, encouraging your intuition and individual preferences to contribute to the design of your feng shui adjustments. One area where we find much flexibility and freedom is in selecting where to superimpose the ba-gua. You may choose to superimpose the ba-gua symbolically over your entire property. Alternatively, you might lay it over your home only, or simply over a number of rooms in your home, or over just one room, or simply over your desktop. You might even choose to do all of these steps. The ba-gua is not a rigid geometric form as much as it is a matrix for the consciousness in matter.

Once you choose the area (most people choose both the entire home and one or two of the rooms used most often), mentally divide it into thirds horizontally and vertically. This will give you nine parts. Some portion of the home, for example, an L-shaped

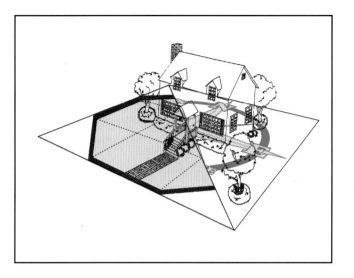

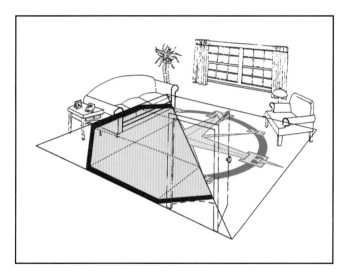

rancher, or a room with a projecting closet, has missing areas in one of the sections, possibly suggesting some missing energy or support for the area of life corresponding to that ba-gua section. Solutions will be presented for these situations in later chapters. You will benefit most by focusing on and adjusting the subtle energies of the areas where you spend most of your time, generally where you sleep and work. Any room in which you spend more than four hours a day should be given close feng shui attention.

The most important aspect of working with the ba-gua is proper alignment. In the Black Hat Tantric Tibetan school of feng shui, the bottom edge of the ba-gua (the line with the doorway) is always aligned in the same direction as the entrance to the area. For example, if you are laying the ba-gua octagon over a piece of property, the entrance would be the driveway, and the bottom of the octagon would overlap the beginning, or approach, of the driveway. For placement over a home, the front door is always used to orient the ba-gua, even if a side or back door is used more often. To lay the ba-gua over a room, the door used most often to enter the room orients the octagon. If you were to superimpose the ba-gua over your desktop, you would align the base of the ba-gua at the area directly in front of where you sit at your desk.

The octagon is an interesting geometric shape, not circular, not square, but an integrated shape somewhere between the two. The internal angles of a standard octagon are 135 degrees. Because that number reduces to a nine ($135 = 1 + 3 + 5 = 9$), one of the most fortunate numbers in feng shui, octagons have energetic significance. The number *9* represents wholeness and completion. As for the eight sides, the number *8* is the same as the symbol for infinity and, when vertical, symbolizes bringing heaven down to earth.

The eight sides of the ba-gua represent the eight important areas of life: family/health, wealth, helpful people/travel, children/creative projects, wisdom/general knowledge, fame/advancement, career, and love.

The Ba-gua Pattern

In Black Hat feng shui, there is a powerful process you can do with the ba-gua called *tracing the nine-star path*. First, simply imagine the layout of the ba-gua over a room you use often; alternatively, you might imagine it over your home. Next, with your attention focused, your energy calm and centered, and your breathing full and slow (deep breathing affects maximum movement of our human chi), look at each of the areas in the order shown on the ba-gua, starting with position 1 and moving through to position 9. Project your chi toward position 1 by directing your attention while breathing fully and rhythmically. Then visualize on the "theater screen" of your mind's eye whatever you might like to have occur in that area of your life. Take the energy from position 1, and with additional focus and intention, address position 2. Follow the same process for the remaining areas.

Position 1, the middle left ninth of the area you are addressing, concerns *Family/Health*. This is the area where you would make a feng shui adjustment to support your family, your health, or a family member's health. Green is the color associated with position 1.

Position 2, the upper left ninth, concerns *Wealth*, representing financial wealth and abundance in general—time, friends, good fortune, and so on. The colors associated with the Wealth area are red, blue, and purple.

Position 3, the center of the ba-gua, is the *Ming Tang* (the reflecting pool) and corresponds to the center of any area over which the ba-gua is placed. Ideally, the central areas of homes or rooms are left relatively open to create an uncrowded, spacious feeling, as this is considered the area where spirit dwells. Yellow is associated with the center.

Position 4, the lower right ninth, is called *Helpful People/Travel*. If you feel the need for some additional helpful people in your life, such as benefactors, mentors, or friends, or if you wish to create more travel in your life or to enhance current travel plans, this is the place to make an adjustment. When traveling, helpful people are quite welcome. The colors for this area are black, white, and gray.

Position 5, the middle right ninth, relates to *Children/Creative Projects*. If any child in your life, including your "inner child," could benefit from some extra support,

use the color white or another feng shui cure in the middle right ninth of the home or in a room in which the child spends a lot of time. This is also a good place to enhance to receive a little extra support if you are beginning a new creative project at home or work. White is associated with this position.

Position 6, the lower left ninth, is called *Wisdom/General Knowledge*. This is an appropriate place to create a study or to store books. Enhancing the knowledge area of life with any of the basic feng shui cures, including color, can help you attract the right teacher, find a helpful book to support growth, or access your inner wisdom. The associated colors are black, blue, and green.

Position 7, the upper middle ninth, relates to *Fame/Advancement*. When you wish to add a burst of energy to your business reputation, red is the color. One's personal reputation can benefit from enhancing this area as well.

Position 8, the lower middle ninth, concerns *Career/Life Journey*. Here we find more gentle support for the advancement of our career and life's journey, not the "firecracker" energy of position 7. An adjustment in this area brings with it more grace and support for the highest unfolding of one's life path. The color is black, only a touch of which is needed.

Position 9, the upper right ninth, is associated with *Romantic Relationship/Marriage*, primarily your love relationship with a significant other, partner, or spouse. The associated colors are red, pink, and white. Adjustment here can help attract a primary relationship into your life or support an existing one. As with all the other positions on the ba-gua, you can choose to work with the associated color(s), or place one of the other energy-stimulating feng shui adjustments in the area.

Although there are eight areas of life, our living spaces are divided into nine sections when looking at the ba-gua of a space. The central square, the Ming Tang, is generally not spoken of as much as the eight outer areas, but it is the main purpose behind the practice of feng shui, that is, to achieve balance by becoming more connected to our center, our spiritual essence.

Interestingly, only this center area, considered the home of spirit, touches all eight areas of life—a reminder that there is a spiritual side to every aspect of life. While decorative adjustments are recommended for the other eight areas, feng shui suggests keeping the central area relatively unadorned and open, allowing room for spirit. This exemplifies the Tao: While it appears to be nothing, it touches and is part of everything.

For additional insight into the workings and influences of the eight areas of life, observe the two areas that fall on either side of an area and consider the ways they affect (or could be more effective in) each part of your life. The Family/Health section is bordered and greatly influenced by the areas representing Wealth on one side and Wisdom/General Knowledge on the other; Wealth is bordered by Fame/Advancement and Family/Health; the Helpful People/Travel area is adjacent to Career/Life Journey and Children/Creative Projects; the Children/Creative Projects area is bordered by Romantic Relationship/Marriage and Helpful People/Travel; Wisdom/General Knowledge is bordered by Career/Life Journey and Family/Health; Fame/Advancement is bordered by Wealth and Romantic Relationship/Marriage; Career/Life Journey is bordered by Helpful People/Travel and Wisdom/General Knowledge; and Romantic Relationship/Marriage is bordered by Fame/Advancement and Children/Creative Projects.

Choosing Colors

Whether through pigment or colored light, our physical, emotional, and psychological states constantly interact with color, one of our most powerful tools. You may choose to work with any of the following systems, or you may prefer to create a personal palette based on the information you learn about your personal feng shui in chapter 11. For the most successful, healing use of color, integrate information from your eyes, mind, and intuition.

Colors Associated with the Five Elements

As discussed earlier, the five elements are metaphors for the different forms and qualities of energy. Color can be used to bring the five elements into your environment.

- The *Fire element* is represented by all shades of red and reddish purple.
- The *Earth element* is represented in all of the colors found in soil around the world: gold, brown, orange, salmon, peach, yellow, copper, bronze, and beige.

- The *Metal element* governs white and silver. Some schools also place shiny gold under the Metal element instead of the Earth element. The Metal element is also present in very light tints of colors.
- The *Water element* is depicted through navy and black, the colors of deepest water. Secondarily, Water constitutes other very dark colors and a dark bluish purple.
- The *Wood element* is found in the colors blue, green, and teal, which are the colors predominantly seen in foliage.

The colors listed above describe the elements in their pure states. Do note, however, that many colors are blends of the five elements. For example, mauve is a combination of red (Fire) and brown (Earth). Any tint of a color requires white (the Metal element). Take pink, for example: Pink is red (Fire) and white (Metal). Any dark shade contains black (Water). A deep, forest green is green (Wood) plus black (Water). Tints support communication. Tones (greyed hues) assist communication and insight, while shades are helpful for insight and reflection.

The Fire element is represented by the color red, the triangular shape, and actual fire. This element invites warmth, inspiration, and passion to the home.

Personal Elements

After completing your personal feng shui information in chapter 11, you will discover your *natal* and *nourishing* elements, as well as any "missing" elements that may not be included in your Five Element Configuration. The *natal element*, a key feng shui focus, is the quality of your *core essence*. The Five Element Configuration, the second personal section to complete in chapter 11, is somewhat representative of your mind and personality. Use the materials, shapes, and colors of your natal and nourishing elements generously in your decor and wardrobe to support your inner essence. Also, use elements that may not be part of your Five Element Configuration for a feeling of completeness, grace, and additional personal support. For balance we crave all five elements. The following poems by Linda Joy Burke and the accompanying illustrations by Linda Montgomery are wonderful interpretations of the energies of the five elements.

Celebrating Veriditas
(for Hildegard von Bingen)

Spring fever's got me watching the
wind direct microcosms.
Pollen blows from here to there,
leaves scatter from late-shedding trees,
to mingle with man-made debris.
Flies and bees awaken
to the sound of the greening,
in the calling, in the echo of the
departing night.
Chronus springs forward.

The white light winter nights
are melting away
and there seems to be
little time for sleeping
with so much to give breath to.

The season is changing,
is greening,
is turning over new leaves
and fresh blossoms of pink,
yellow and white,
and sending out its message,
through the sound
of day-long rainfalls,
through the scent of
freshly-mown perfume,
and royal green blades upright glow.

—*Linda Joy Burke*

w o o d

29

Fire

I am a sunbeam glinting and sparkling
on a clear water pond at dawn
the bearer of energy and warmth
blazing into high noon on a summer lawn.
I can engulf you in my flaming
scorch or pierce you to the core.
I am the passage of deep burnings
clarifying the spirit forevermore.
I dance the dance of immortality
Prometheus unbound,
I will fill your sight with a glowing
your ears with a crackling sound.
I am the cozy warmth in the window seat nook
the hearth side in the winter,
the raging of a bonfire
a birthday candle's flicker.
I am the echo of laughter at gatherings
the grin, the wink, the smile,
the great transformer and lover,
wild and beautiful all the while.
I am the burning in the passion of a lover's kiss
the flicker of joy in her eyes
fuser of lover and beloved
lightning flashing from the skies.

I am a fever raging and sweating
a heartbeat throbbing on,
a dynamic vital force
drumming out an ardent song.
I am spitting searing lava,
an inspiration bursting from the soul,
a luminous magenta sunset
a pile of red hot coal.
I am a violent unfettered thing,
a light that will not expire,
a deep dark red red rose
a brilliant star,
I am fire!

—*Linda Joy Burke*

fire

Harvesting Tenderness

Part I

While I was driving through
the neighboring farmland
I could see how all those
empty well-tilled fields had yielded
sweet corn, beans, tomatoes, cabbage,
kohlrabi, squash, and blackberries . . .
and where there weren't fruit and
vegetables,
there was the sight and lingering scent
of roses, portulaca,
zinnias, sunflowers, gladiolus, and
lavender nicotiana . . .
There were signs up everywhere
advertising herbs, and honey,
and rhubarb, and fresh eggs . . . it was
a good year here for farming,
just enough fire and water
to keep the wood in the earth
moving upward to meet the heavens.

Part II

Soon I know this summer will end
and the flaming will turn to cadmium
and rust,
and the pale auras of the
golden glistenings will
fall into place,
but not now, not just yet.
It's only the time to think
about letting go.
More the time of celebrating harvest
and receiving nurturing from
this inner and outer earth
more the time of being the change
rather than preparing for the change,
it seems more the time of
touching the earth as she touches
the earth in me,
it seems more a time of
learning how to be tender . . .

—*Linda Joy Burke*

While Driving to Work
the Mind Tends to Wonder

Part I

If my skin turns to bumping goose flesh
on these heavily dewed mornings
I cannot remain forlorn
even though I know there are warnings
of when the blue black
in an evening sky
will without a sound
push cold leaves dying
snow flurries flying
into a winter's ground.

Part II

It is such an exquisite luxury
for these wistful eyes to see
this effusive luscious autumn
this flaming within great trees,
moving green within them back
into the brown blood of the earth
back to wondrousness
a subtle joyousness
back to live before birth.
Red aura of maples
branches of green, yellow and orange
in singular trees,
force my breath to quicken
I feel my spirit lighten
like the notes of a reed.

Within the thickening sap of autumn
leaves open my eyes.
God what an immediate
intensely gratifying
illuminating surprise.

Part III

In autumn, after brilliance
there is melancholy
the deep sigh of an elder
letting go at last
of the weight
of a long and fruitful life.
In autumn, after the falling
there is the browning,
after the browning
there is the raking,
after the raking,
there is the burying
of this season away.

—*Linda Joy Burke*

35

I Am the World of
Waters Wild

I am what comes
from a thousand raindrops and mist,
and a thousand dew drops, and glacier.
I am creek and stream
and a thousand rivers,
sea, and ocean, and a thousand tears.
I am the trickle, the whoosh and
the rush and splash. I am the spilling
and receding, transporting and breeding
of a thousand creatures,
with a thousand fears,
and I carry an ancestral message
spanning thousands of years.

I am the puddles and falls,
and a thousand lakes,
I am the embryonic fluid
and a thousand snow flakes,
I'm the marsh and the cove,
and a thousand baptisms.
I am the ripple, the ebb
and the wave, and flow.
I'm the cleansing, and the releasing,
the cooling and nourishing,
of a thousand creatures,
with a thousand fears,
and I carry an ancestral message
spanning thousands of years.

As I move down to rest deep
in a thousand frigid white light winter nights,
I conform, in a change born
from what surrounds me,
sometimes I can't be so free,
yet still I bring a thousand delights,
to a thousand creatures,
with a thousand fears,
and I carry an ancestral message
spanning thousands of years.

As I shake off the stillness
of my solid form
with the courage and the strength
of the spiritually reborn,
I am a thousand tides
penetrating, and emerging from
the briny deep,
I am transient and adaptable
to the shores that keep
me moving and creating a home,
for thousands of carp, and whale,
and snake, and shale,
for thousands of cells and emotions
that well from thousands of
creatures, with thousands of fears,
and I carry an ancestral message
spanning thousands of years.

—*Linda Joy Burke*

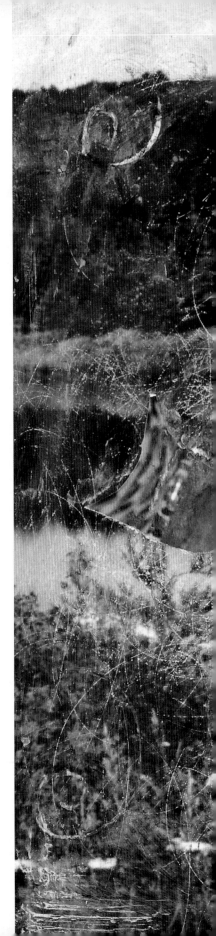

36

Color Triads

A wonderful way to produce an incredible feeling of harmony is to compose your primary color scheme of three colors from elements that border each other in either the nourishing cycle (the *sheng* sequence) or in the control cycle (the *ke* sequence). The sheng cycle is the nourishing, generative force of growth in nature. However, if we had only the sheng cycle, there would be no equilibrium. The fact that water extinguishes fire is a beneficial example of the control, or ke, cycle by which elements are tempered and healthy boundaries are created.

Using an odd number of colors in your decorating plan creates a dynamic, creative scheme. For example, pale gray (Metal) walls and draperies, with navy (Water), gray, and medium blue (Wood) upholstery, follows the nourishing cycle in the predominant colors of the decor. By adding small accents of flowers in the colors rose (Fire) and yellow (Earth), the room emits the feeling of completeness, having all five elements represented.

The Nourishing Cycle

Water⟶ Wood ⟶ Fire⟶ Earth⟶ Metal⟶ (back to Water)

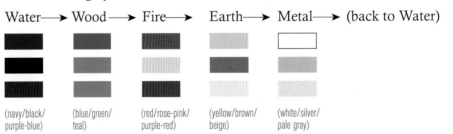

(navy/black/ purple-blue)   (blue/green/ teal)   (red/rose-pink/ purple-red)   (yellow/brown/ beige)   (white/silver/ pale gray)

A living room with a black (Water) sofa and love seat, red (Fire) area rug and chair, and white (Metal) walls has a streamlined, crisp, contained feel to it, exemplary of the control cycle. The word *control* often has a negative connotation; however, understood through the Five Element Theory, control is quite helpful and necessary, keeping balance by setting limits.

The Control Cycle

Water⟶ Fire⟶ Metal ⟶ Wood ⟶Earth⟶ (back to Water)

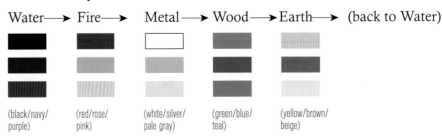

(black/navy/ purple)   (red/rose/ pink)   (white/silver/ pale gray)   (green/blue/ teal)   (yellow/brown/ beige)

The Eight Compass Directions, Associated Elements, and Colors

In feng shui, your home is of paramount importance because it surrounds the center of your universe—your body-mind-spirit. Compass readings taken from the center of your home can tell you how the five elements energetically align in each room. Each compass direction is governed by a particular element.

Stand near the center of your home and, using a compass, determine the orientation of the four cardinal points—north, south, east, west—and the four directions in between—northwest, southwest, northeast, and southeast—in your home. Divide your home into thirds from front to back and, again, from side to side, as was done with the ba-gua pattern. This yields nine sections, with you standing at or near the central ninth. (The same grid applies to the other floors of your home.)

With your home divided into nine sections, each room will fall either completely under one of the eight primary directions or will be split between two or three of the directions, depending on the orientation of your home and the size of the room. For example, a room that spans across the front or back of a home will involve three of the nine divisions. For very long rooms, work with the various element requirements for each area, depending on its compass direction/element. The center ninth of your home always falls under the Earth element. The other eight directions are under the influences of the elements as follows:

North:	Water element	Northwest:	Metal element
South:	Fire element	Southwest:	Earth element
East:	Wood element	Northeast:	Earth element
West:	Metal element	Southeast:	Wood element

List each room in your home, its direction(s) on the compass, and the element(s) governing the room's direction(s), as shown on the above chart. This information is the room's natal element. Decorating a room in accordance with its natal element and/or its nourishing element—the element preceding this natal element in the nourishing cycle, as seen in the nourishing cycle diagram in chapter 1—adds feelings of harmony and subtle well-being to a room.

If the element ruling a room happens to be your personal control element (see chapter 11), you can create more balance by bringing into the room its own control element. This step creates a control for your control, making the room feel more comfortable by giving your natal element some "breathing room." For example, let's say you are born under the Wood element and your living room is in the west or northwest, which places it under the Metal element. Because Metal (the room's natal element) controls Wood (your natal element), bringing in some of the Fire element (which controls Metal) will create some energetic space for your natal Wood element to flourish.

Flexibility is necessary when working with these "rules." Sometimes we can benefit from having our controlling element included, to balance out a present imbalance—a decision that requires self-knowledge, good intuition, a review of the emotional qualities of the five elements and what you might feel you need, or the guidance of a five-element practitioner such as a shiatsu therapist, an acupuncturist, or a feng shui practitioner. Generally, decorating decisions should include your natal and/or nourishing elements for an extraordinary amount of personal energy support.

When a room is regularly used by a few people, create a decorating palette that addresses everyone's needs, bringing in, as warranted, natal or nourishing

The nourishing cycle.
Yellow walls/Earth element, nourish the
white color of the comforter/Metal
element, which, in turn, nourishes the
dark tones in the bed skirt and
pillows/Water element.

colors or materials, any missing elements, and balance to any control-element rooms. A general rule of thumb for rooms used by larger groups is to include all five elements, covering everyone's needs, while using colors on the lighter side. White (present in lighter colors) adds the Metal element, which is helpful for communication.

There are no clear percentages on the amount of an element recommended when decorating a room. As you become more familiar with identifying the five elements in your environment and understanding your own natal and nourishing elements, your intuition will guide you in finding the right balance. Interestingly, numerous schools of thought and even conflicting information about both feng shui and Chinese cosmology are likely the products of practitioners and teachers conveying their unique methods and integrating individual discoveries.

The Nine Basic Feng Shui Cures

The following collection of feng shui cures are taken from the Black Hat Sect of Tantric Buddhism. While some situations respond best to certain adjustments, for the most part the cures can be used interchangeably. Think of the cures as "acupuncture needles" used inside and outside your home to adjust areas; to speed up, slow down, or raise the movement of chi; or to enhance any of the eight areas of your life shown on the ba-gua.

Physicists have proved that light, color, and sound move in visible and invisible wavelengths of energy. We benefit from the physical beauty of these cures, as the invisible and visible waves carry chi along and act as our first three feng shui adjustment methods.

1. *Reflective objects.* Lights, mirrors, and faceted leaded-glass crystals increase or reflect light (energy).

2. *Sound.* The vibrations of music, wind chimes, and bells move and circulate chi.

3. *Color.* Seen as pure energy, color is used to bring the five elements, balance, and vitality to rooms.

4. *Living objects.* Flowers, plants, bonsai, and aquariums have a strong life force that raises the overall chi in a room; they may also be used to augment one of the eight positions of the ba-gua.

Above, top
An octagon surrounded by the eight tri-grams (three-lined patterns) of the I Ching is a powerful image that is used to attract positive chi and repel negativity.

Above, bottom
Wind chimes move chi with the invisible sound wavelengths of various notes and tones.

5. *Electrically powered items.* As electricity circulates through commonplace items such as computers, televisions, and stereos, it adds to the amount of energy circulating in the area of the ba-gua in which the electronic item is placed.

6. *Bamboo items.* Bamboo is a highly revered plant in the East, providing food, tatami mat floor covering, curtains, beautiful plants, and musical instruments. The plants, curtains, and flutes are used to raise and moderate chi.

7. *Moving items.* It is easy to understand how water fountains, mobiles, and other objects with motion encourage the movement of chi.

8. *Heavy objects.* To help create more stability and groundedness in a room or in an area of your life, heavy objects such as furniture, statues, and stones may be purposely placed in significant positions according to the ba-gua.

9. *Others.* This category, feng shui master Professor Thomas Lin Yun teaches, is the largest category of feng shui cures. Basically, any item you own that you really love can be considered a feng shui cure because a cure is more about your connection to an item than it is about the item itself. Beloved gifts, favorite possessions, memorabilia, and inherited belongings may be placed in meaningful positions to act as feng shui adjustments. Also in this category are items for special use—red ribbons, firecrackers, and personal cures.

In feng shui, the color red is associated with joy and exuberance. Red ribbon cut in any increment of nine inches (nine, eighteen, and so forth) is suggested for hanging feng shui cures such as crystals or flutes. While it is not imperative that you use red cording or ribbon—for example, you may use fishing line, nylon, or thin wire, if you prefer—it does add more energy. Firecrackers use sound to blow out stagnant chi or residual chi from previous occupants or previous negative events.

In the following chapters, you will discover many ways to use these and other physical, mundane feng shui cures. (*Mundane cures* are any of the material adjustments you make to your physical environment.) Professor Lin Yun believes that physical cures hold a small amount of power in their overall effectiveness. The true strength lies in the transcendental cures, which—Professor Lin Yun jokingly, but poignantly, teaches in every one of his lectures—hold 140 percent of the effectiveness, emphasizing the importance of rituals and the power of the images we hold in our minds.

Feng shui supports you holistically—body, mind, and spirit. The physical, mundane cures are a great beginning: They adjust your surroundings for greater physical comfort, mental reminders, and spiritual inspiration. The work truly begins, however, when we inspirit our surroundings through the rituals of transcendental cures: clearing the space, raising the chi, and employing creative visualization. (An example of the powerful process of transcendental cures is included in chapter 6.)

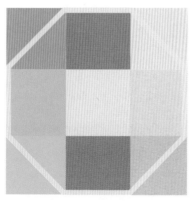

Candlewood
Clarkdale, Arizona

Space is the breath of art.
—Frank Lloyd Wright, *Architect*

This is simply unbelievable, I think as I drive up the winding path toward the beautiful, sprawling stone and stucco home known as Candlewood. It appears to grow right out of the earth, inviting me to journey inside. Frank Lloyd Wright would be proud.

First Impressions

A great midwinter escape, I am at the home of Andrea and Rennie and their children, Emmanuel and Maya, in Clarkdale, Arizona, 2,400 miles away from the January snow and gray winter skies of my native Baltimore. The warmth and unique terrain of the desert fifteen miles outside Sedona, Arizona, make the forty acres surrounding Candlewood spectacular: The living topography here is awe-inspiring.

Above
Having mountains at its back and on both sides and a gentle downward slope at its front surrounds Candlewood in the protective "armchair" position.

According to feng shui, hills and valleys, mountains and ridges are visible formations caused by the invisible, underlying energetic forces of nature. The varied, undulating outline of the landforms indicates a great deal of chi energy, especially land-based chi, sometimes referred to as "dragon energy" or "dragon blood," the dragon being the supreme creature in Chinese mythology. Hills and mountains are called "dragon veins" in respect to the coursing of life-giving chi through the land and its relationship to the nutrient- and oxygen-rich blood that is carried by the veins throughout animal and human bodies. Mountain ranges are often studied for symbolic animal forms, which indicate the type of energy present.

Strengths and Weaknesses

Several aspects of the site work well and noticeably affect the feng shui. One strength of Andrea and Rennie's property is its expansive size. Forty acres gives them a lot of room to create a very natural, embracing environment. The front of their home has a beautiful balance of yin/yang features: straight, rectilinear lines (yang) complement curved columns and curving walkways (yin). The windmill in front of the home—not something you see every day!—is a wonderful catalyst to attract and move chi energy. The home backs up to and is flanked by mountains in an "armchair position." The mountains shelter the home, providing a sense of stability and security for the inhabitants. A particularly fortunate feature is the home's southern fronting, the luckiest possible direction in which a home can be situated, according to the form and Black Hat schools of feng shui. The long, curving driveway leads to a meandering walkway. This arrangement benefits the inhabitants by allowing the chi to approach the home gently, providing a feeling of unhurried grace. (Many homes have walkways that are "straight arrows," or *sha* [unbalanced, rushing chi; also called "secret arrows"] leading directly from the sidewalk or driveway to the home. In such cases, to visually break the straight line pointing toward the front door, evergreens and red flowers might be planted in a random pattern on either side of the walkway. The slower wavelengths present in red will slow the movement of chi, whether the color is incorporated through the use of flowers or a functional or decorative item. Red also attracts human chi [one's attention] well. A mirror or wind chimes hanging just outside the front door also work to deflect some of the *sha*.)

To categorize its shape, we walked around the exterior of Candlewood, which falls under the Water element: Its shape resembles a meandering stream, with undulating forms throughout. Having established Five Element Configurations for each member of the family, it was clear Andrea and her sixteen-year-old son, Emmanuel, were comfortable, both being born under the Water element. Maya, a twenty-one-year-old college student born under the Wood element, is also at ease here, as Water (rain) nourishes Wood (plants and trees). Rennie, on the other hand, was born under the Earth element, which controls the Water element, just as river banks give shape to the rivers. Therefore, for him, the Water element of his home is energetically draining. His core energy, Earth, is at odds and in a control cycle with his home. (See chapters 1 and 2 for more on the control cycle and chapter 11 for detailed information on the five elements.) We will increase the harmony at Candlewood through both interior and exterior feng shui remedies.

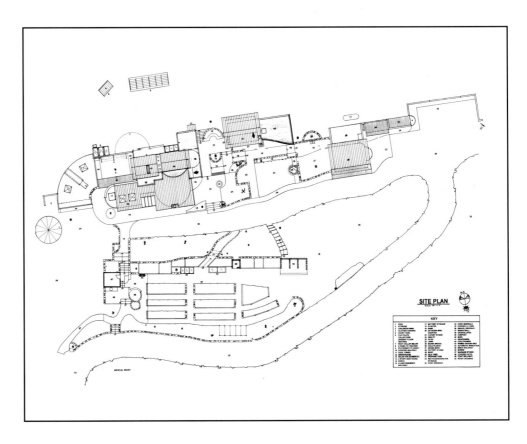

SITE PLAN

Getting Started

At the beginning of every consultation, I share information from the feng shui chart that I prepare previously for each inhabitant. I also show a diagram of the ba-gua so everyone may see where the eight areas of life fall in their home. At this point, to gain some feng shui "clues," I am always eager to hear what it is like to live in that home.

Rennie and Andrea have several concerns. Rennie says, "As wonderful as our home is, it's a lot of responsibility. We'd like it to flow better—to keep it all together." Andrea mentions her constant struggle to maintain the garden, as it provides about eighty percent of the produce for this vegetarian family. There is also a vacant caretaker's house on the property, awaiting a helpful occupant.

Feng Shui Clues

The door at this home reminds me that our environments frequently give us not-so-subtle clues as to how we can improve our lives. A woman in Baltimore told me she wanted to have a busier social life and more drop-in company. On arriving at her home, I rang the doorbell and waited. After ringing again and still receiving no response, I knocked on the door. When she finally answered, the door opened only about eighteen inches. I struggled to get inside, carrying my briefcase and a satchel of supplies. She told me that over the years her 100-year-old townhouse had settled unevenly and that the hardwood floor allowed the door to open only so far. On top of that, her doorbell was out of order. I explained why doorways deserve close attention. She had the front door planed, so it could open fully, and she had the doorbell repaired. Now she has an easier time inviting guests, and she even knows when they've arrived!

The Importance of Entrances

A doorway or entranceway is one of the *most* important areas in feng shui. The doorway is a threshold between our outer, more active, yang encounter with the world, and our inner, more private, yin experience in the world, where we rest, relax, and formulate ideas for the realization of our life goals. In this key position, it is critical that everything be in good working order. Each time we enter a home, we receive a first impression; ideally it is one of welcoming comfort, beauty, and order.

A few problems greet me at the front door. For one, it does not stay open. Rennie tells me they have a doorstop to keep the door open, but this is an insufficient cure. The hinges should be adjusted or the door rehung: whatever it takes to make the repair. The symbology of the door constantly closing halfway represents a limit to the amount of chi energy allowed to enter the home. Candlewood is the third house this couple has built for themselves, and they now seek a little more ease in life. By putting the front door in good working order, they will invite more chi energy into their lives, which may manifest as improved physical energy, better health, increased opportunities in life, or increased wealth.

Nothing Broken

There is another problem with the front door: The glass is broken. The custom-cut piece of glass for this specially designed door broke on installation. It's been damaged for about five years, constantly affecting the chi as it enters the house. One of the cardinal rules in feng shui is *have nothing broken!* The chi energy of a broken item diminishes the vibrant energy of everything around it. The chi entering this home will be more vital after the glass and door are repaired.

Main Entrance

Based on their personal feng shui charts and the pa-kua system (see chapter 11), the front door facing east nourishes Andrea, but it does little for Rennie. Hanging a mirror to reflect an image of the door to the north, one of Rennie's better directions, helps matters.

This unique red column draws chi energy and attention to the front door.

Inside the front door, the left wall extends out into a corridor that leads from the front door to the back door. Consequently, when you walk in, your left eye focuses on the wall, and your right views the corridor. These differing depths of view set up a disconcerting split in one's field of vision, disrupting the balance between the left and right sides of the brain. (The right eye goes to the left side of the brain, while the left eye goes to the right.) Hanging a mirror near the edge of the left wall in the entry will allow the left eye to experience more depth through the mirror, and so will solve the problem by expanding the field of vision.

The column in front of the home, being the same color as the house, currently gets lost. Originally intended to be a strong accent in the home's design, the column will be decorated with a mural of reds, purples, blues, and greens, creating a nice focal point and highlighting an outstanding design feature.

It is generally recommended that something red be placed on or near the front door, or toward the front of the house, to attract more chi. Many front doors are painted red or a strong accent color for this very reason. Red flowers or a red welcome mat are other ways to invite more chi. Rennie, born under the Earth element, will especially benefit from the nourishing Fire element he sees in the red as he approaches his home.

Water near the front door also attracts chi and invites wealth. (In China, *feng,* the slang word for money, means water.) Having the Water element located near the front of the home will speak to Andrea and Emmanuel in particular, as their natal element is Water. On hearing this suggestion, and being a ceramist, Andrea immediately felt inspired to make a ceramic water fountain to catch rainwater from their downspout. Already more chi is flowing!

Let's Go Inside

As we enter their home, I explain to Andrea and Rennie that feng shui seeks to increase the vitality of our living spaces, surrounding us with harmonious design elements to create more growth, balance, and abundance in the many areas of our lives: Family/Health, Wealth, Spiritual Connection, Helpful People/Travel, Children/Creative Projects, Wisdom/General Knowledge, Fame/Advancement, Career/Life Journey, and Romantic Relationship/Marriage. (See chapter 2 for information on the ba-gua pattern.)

As I imagine the ba-gua over the home, I find that the living room falls under the area related to Family/Health. The far left ninth of their home, the Wealth position, is missing. To remedy this, a greenhouse will be built in this area, a fabulous plan as plants represent and stimulate growth in all areas of the ba-gua. There will be much activity and constant movement in the greenhouse/Wealth area, as everyone in the family loves to garden. Because the plants will bring lots of greenery into the Wealth area, the other colors of the Wealth area—red, purple, and blue—should be incorporated either in the shelving or the pots for the plants.

A bathroom sits in the Fame/Advancement area. A hanging plant strategically placed over the toilet will allow the Fame/Advancement area to gather energy. Plants have a living, energetic field that adds chi to any area in which they are placed. Red, the color symbolically associated with the Fame area, is also recommended for this bathroom. A touch of rose or red and a large green plant will complement this room's existing teal tiles and white paint nicely.

Utility Rooms Benefit from Beauty, Too

A utility room is located on the other side of the bathroom, between the Fame/Advancement and Romantic Relationship/Marriage areas. A piece of artwork that speaks to both Andrea and Rennie will enhance an empty wall on the edge of the Marriage area. Artwork making use of the colors red, white, and pink will amplify the potency of this feng shui adjustment. In the Romantic Relationship/Marriage area, red is associated with passion, white with communication, and pink with universal love. In a home, energy is moved around most by human chi. In areas where little time is spent, beautiful items and/or symbolic colors provide other ways to improve the chi, or life energy, in an area.

In the upper-right ninth of this home, there is a circular root cellar. The circular shape represents heaven here in the Marriage position. Because they are in the Marriage area, the root cellar and utility room must be kept orderly. Old belongings pile up easily when stored, creating stagnant energy. Keeping only the things that you like, that are in good repair, and that you will use creates some extra space and lightens the feeling of an area. After Andrea and Rennie clean out and organize their storage areas, the new space will allow room for growth and inspiration to re-enter their beautiful committed relationship.

Touches of beauty enhance the strictly utilitarian aspect of storage rooms. For example, using decorative baskets or special glass canning jars to hold food in a root cellar will bring us joy and improve the time we spend in this work-related area.

As we come around the ba-gua, we find the pantry in the Helpful People/Travel position. This area is extremely functional and holds a lot of food and equipment. The pantry stays organized, despite its frequent use, much to the wonderment of Andrea. Order, which is of paramount importance in feng shui, supports a smooth, rhythmic, abundant flow of chi. Like the pantry, the lives of the family members are indeed well-stocked. Rennie, an architect, and Andrea, a ceramist, dancer, and massage therapist have many friends and clients (helpful people) in their businesses, and their children also enjoy numerous friends.

Cooking with Chi

The kitchen is partly in the Helpful People/Travel area and partially in the Career/Life Journey area. The color for Career/Life Journey is black; the colors for Helpful People/Travel are black, gray, and white. The kitchen, with its white walls and gray floor, is accented by touches of black in the rug and in the brackets holding plants. Two hanging plants bring in a touch of living nature, positively affecting the chi in the kitchen Career/Life Journey area. A faceted leaded-glass crystal hanging in the windows will further increase and move the energy of the Career/Life Journey area.

The stove rests against a solid wall and not under a window, both desirable features. In feng shui, the stove is an extremely important part of the home. Chi should be accumulated in the stove area, the place where nourishing food, which contributes to the health of the family, is prepared. In this home, the stove is not in a direct line with the sink, again a desirable feature, as it avoids a clash between the Fire and Water elements. The "mouth of the stove" (the oven door) faces north, which is good for Andrea but suggests a needed adjustment for Rennie. A small mirror hung on the wall can pull an image of part of the front of the oven to one of Rennie's best directions, a simple cure. Rennie enjoys cooking and spends time in the kitchen, but even if he didn't, it would be important to align the kitchen energies with the elemental energies portrayed in his personal chart.

Balancing Chi in the Living Room

In the living room, there are many windows, making furniture arrangement quite difficult. Ideally, one would not have one's back to a window or an entrance; however, this is somewhat unavoidable in this room. To create a feeling of protection behind the back of one's head, we make use of stained glass and plants. The living room is sunken, a feature not recommended in feng shui. Elevating chi is a main focus of feng shui and sunken rooms move too much chi down-

The sofa no longer blocks the door. With no solid walls in front of which to place the sofa, plants, a floor lamp, and window blinds create a symbolic backing.

ward. Floor lamps with their upward-shining light, and plants help to raise and balance the chi, as do the tall windows and hanging plants. Where our attention is led, chi generally follows.

The living room was purposefully oriented to the south, so it might act as a passive source of solar heat and light for the home. The south is governed by the Fire element, making it beneficial for Rennie to spend time here in his nourishing element. For Andrea and Emmanuel, the Fire element can be somewhat draining, as their natal element, Water, controls fire. To balance this, sources of the Water element should be added—water in a fountain, an aquarium, or a clear vase holding water and flowers are a few examples. Another option would be to add light touches of navy or black, the colors of the Water element, to the room. With its southern orientation, this room has so much of the Fire element that adding these touches of water will not diminish the nourishing benefits the room holds for Rennie.

The position of the ba-gua octagon covering the living room is Wisdom/General Knowledge. The energies of the room nicely support study and philosophic conversations to deepen wisdom.

Bolstering the Ming Tang

The dining room is located in the center of their home. The center, or Ming Tang, is considered the place where spirit dwells the most. The fireplace in the dining room, when not in use, might be considered an empty artery. When the flue is shut, it's just a cut-out rectangle or passage within the home, with little energy moving through it. This may be one reason mirrors have become popular as decorative items for mantles. Symbolically they let energy move through the open chimney space and double the light/energy of the area.

Other solutions for the fireplace might be to use bright, reflective doors, perhaps with dark glass, that almost act as mirrors. Wide brass trim on fireplace doors is a favorable reflective surface that increases and moves chi. Other possible fireplace adjustments include a beautiful, painted screen showing a landscape, or a bright, floral design to sit in front of the fireplace opening. You might even choose to place a beautiful arrangement of colorful candles or green plants in front of the fireplace. Still, a mirror, even a small one, is one of the best fireplace adjustments. If a wall mirror is not desired, consider using a small, mirrored pedestal base for an art object on the mantle, or a larger mirrored pedestal for a plant on the floor in front of the fireplace.

Capturing Chi for Recirculation

The hallway goes from the front door to the back door in a straight line and allows far too much chi to pass directly through the home without circulating in each room, as is preferred. To counter this effect, we have a ba-gua mirror (an octagonal mirror with the eight trigrams of the *I Ching*) above the back door to reflect some of the chi back into the house before it has a chance to exit. A red runner placed on the floor of the hallway can help slow the energy down a bit and ground it, before it goes out the back door. Chi pooled on the first floor has greater opportunity to fill the main floor of the house, enhancing the areas where the family spends most of its time together, before going upstairs to circulate through the second floor. A moving item such as a mobile or a leaded-glass crystal might be hung in the hallway, as well, to help interrupt and circulate some of the chi on its journey down the hall.

When the front and rear doors of a home line up with each other, diversions must be created to keep chi from rushing through. In this example, the red runner on the floor, the ba-gua suspended over the back door, and the plants and Balinese carved figurine hanging from the beam all provide such diversions.

The stairway leading to the second floor is steep, and a window is located at the top, pulling chi up the stairs toward the window. This creates a subtle feeling of imbalance. To counter this feeling, richly colored runners on the stair treads or artwork on the adjacent wall (creating an eye-level focal point) will help balance and ground the movement of chi energy in this location.

Just outside the master bedroom is the perfect spot to place imagery representing a happy couple.

Harmonious Aspects for the Master Bedroom

The entrance to the master bedroom has a delightful, hand-painted batik wall hanging, depicting two dancing, happy figures—a sign of joyful energy. The master bedroom is located in the southeast corner of the home, in the Wood element. This location may be a bit draining for Andrea's Water element and somewhat controlling for Rennie's natal Earth element. Bringing more of the Water and Earth elements into the bedroom will balance the energy for both of them.

Across from the foot of the bed, there is a series of mirrors between the windows. Mirrors at the head or foot of the bed are not recommended, as some believe that our souls leave our bodies when we go to sleep and return before we awaken and they should not be reflected in a mirror. In feng shui, this is the prime consideration for not placing mirrors across from the foot of the bed. Also, a reflection at the head or foot of a bed could create a startled feeling on waking. Rennie placed the mirrors between the bedroom windows to bridge the windows and to create an open feeling on the wall. To achieve a similar, but more favorable, effect, plants or a mural replicating the mountain line visible from the bed are possible options.

A touch of red (Fire element) is also recommended for the bedroom. This will figuratively "burn up" some of the Wood energy, making the bedroom more comfortable. The head of the bed is placed well for Andrea, but not so well for Rennie. A small octagonal or oval mirror, placed off to the right side of the bed near the fireplace, will pull part of Rennie's image to the southwest, one of his best directions. Oval mirrors are often used in bedrooms to amplify conjugal bliss.

A Beam over the Bed

In the bedroom, a beam spans the width of the bed, which may cause ill health in the area of the body the beam crosses. Rennie has severe and, at times, debilitating lower back pain, which, not coincidentally, is the area of his body directly under the beam. Relocating the bed is not an option, as the only alternative direction is not favorable for Andrea or Rennie. Concealing the beam, perhaps with fabric, or painting the beam a very light color might help reflect light and chi around the beam. Andrea and Rennie decide to hang fabric over the bed, like a canopy, to obscure the beam and its negative energy. A traditional adjustment for beams involves hanging a pair of bamboo flutes on a diagonal, mouthpieces at the lowered ends, to create the top of the ba-gua octagon. This simple method breaks the straight line of the beam and funnels chi upward through the flutes.

I told Rennie of a transcendental, metaphysical feng shui cure for backaches, which he tried and reported some success. Under his bed, in the area of his backache, he placed nine pieces of chalk in a bowl of uncooked rice. After blessing the bowl with the three transcendental cures, he left the bowl in place for nine nights. If the pain persisted, he was instructed to change the rice and chalk and

Above, left–before:

This support beam holds the weight of the roof. Pressure is exerted under the beam, while chi is blocked on both sides where the beam meets the ceiling.

Above, right–after:

Chi now rolls across the fabric canopy, and the flute further disperses the beam's pressure. On the far beam, the plant's own energy field effectively moves chi along.

repeat for a total of twenty-seven nights. (This and other transcendental cures and rituals are described in *Living Color* by Sarah Rossbach and Master Lin Yun.)

Areas of Creativity and Inspiration

The second floor has a sewing room and a meditation room. Andrea is a dancer and a creative seamstress, so she designs many of her performance outfits. In the sewing room, Andrea has a wonderful opportunity to bring in a lot of her personal chart, as she uses this space exclusively. Born under the yang Water element and having a lot of yang influence in her Five Element Configuration, Andrea needs to increase the yin for balance and to focus the feminine energy in this area with darker, diffuse colors. This will produce a cozy space in which she can draw from her inner creativity. Other yin touches might include sheer lace panels, which diffuse light (yang), for the French doors, flowers in clear vases, and more cool-toned blues and greens in plants, planters, and paint colors.

The meditation room is located in the Romantic Relationship/Marriage area of the ba-gua. There is a lovely altar here, decorated with flowers, photographs, and symbolic, meaningful items. Every home should have a small shrine in a private area, somewhere not visible from the front door. This nourishes and supports the spiritual aspects of our lives.

Feng Shui Acknowledges Our Deepest Selves

After this feng shui reading, we gathered in the dining room. Rennie, who is an architect and craftsman, is fascinated by this unique way of approaching the integration of spirituality, space, and design. Andrea and Rennie are quite moved by the depth of feng shui. Andrea got chills as she shared that she has come across few things in life that go to a level this meaningful. She felt "acknowledged and seen." The triad connecting feng shui, one's home, and one's spirit is the essential substance we create in every project.

The moongate window in one wall of the greenhouse was created especially to frame the beautiful natural view, which changes with the seasons.

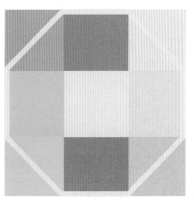

Pre-War Home
Surrey, England

Harmony—the existence of balance, beauty, spontaneity, and creativity.
—Harriet Beinfield and Efrem Korngold, *Acupuncurists, Authors*

This five-bedroom stucco home is placed in one of the best locations for a positive site, according to feng shui: It is approximately a third of the way down a hill, shielded from the forces of wind and weather.

The red door serves many functions. It symbolizes the red phoenix, the spiritual force at the front of a home depicting inspiration and renewal. It repels negativity, grabs attention to lead chi to the house, and serves as a focal point—a bright accent announcing to visitors the location of the front entrance, the mouth of chi.

An "Accidental" Meeting

While browsing through the feng shui titles in a bookstore, I struck up a conversation on the subject with Jane. She previously had a feng shui consultation and thought it might be time for another. I, relishing thoughts of the beautiful architecture I had found so familiar and comfortable since arriving in England, volunteered to help.

Jane wanted a consultation for two reasons: (1) to create as much support as possible for each member of her family, and (2) to address some health issues. Jane and her husband Peter have three sons, two of whom are entering adolescence. She hopes a feng shui adjustment will help Ben, Chris, and Tom embrace their individuality, support their self-esteem, and create maximum family harmony. Chris has a chronic, painful ear problem that is affecting his ability to learn in school. There is a strong relationship between the senses and the five elements, and I hope that the adjustment we make will help him.

House History

The attention-getting red door helps to lead chi into the house.

It pays to know what you are stepping into, what you unknowingly may be inheriting when you move into a house. Ask a lot of questions: How was the health of the previous owners? Why did they sell the house? Have divorces or deaths occurred in the home? Answers to these questions can give you insight into the feng shui of a home. Ideally, the previous home owner will have sold because of some good fortune: a promotion at work, perhaps, or the desire for a larger house. Oftentimes, however, homes come with a negative history. Owners may have been forced to sell because of injury, demotion, bankruptcy, or divorce. Each of the materials used to build a home has its own energy field—the place where chi resides. This field is affected, positively or negatively, by what occurs in its vicinity. When buying a home, you may want to choose one with a positive history. At the very least, plan to do some clearing rituals to remove any leftover, unfortunate chi.

This home was built in the 1920s. For two years, the house sat empty as the previous residents of twenty years, both doctors, attempted to sell it to finance their retirement. To attract a buyer, the sellers were prepared to gut the dated

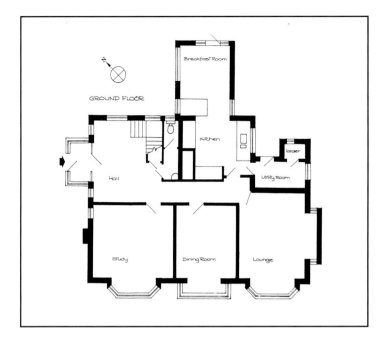

GROUND FLOOR

Breakfast Room

Kitchen

larder

Hall

Utility Room

Study

Dining Room

Lounge

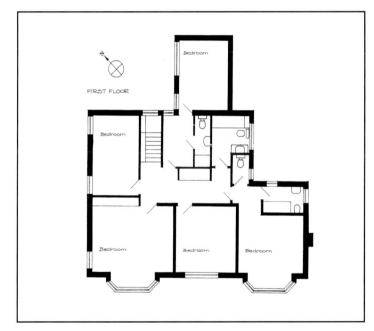

FIRST FLOOR

Bedroom

Bedroom

Bedroom

Bedroom

Bedroom

interior and to totally remodel in accordance with the buyer's wishes. On seeing this, Jane and Peter felt they had found their dream home. They bought the house; then the problems began. There were construction delays, and contractors attempted to substitute cheap building materials. These and myriad other problems created a tense, antagonistic relationship among all parties. Finally, after months of work and five months of arguments with the sellers, Jane and Peter were ready to move in.

The renovation process removed a lot of the energy left over from previous residents. Old patterns and memories were carted away. New flooring, tiles, and finishes provided a fresh start for Jane and Peter. Because the structure of the home was not changed, the soul of the place was maintained. To clear away any remaining residual negative chi and to start with an energetic "clean slate," we set off nine firecrackers in the doorway, tossing them from inside the house out onto the porch. In feng shui, this is called a clearing ritual. We further deepened this ritual with the three transcendental cures (see chapter 6), and then were ready to address the more mundane, physical feng shui.

The Bathroom as the First Impression

This lovely home has a problem as soon as you enter the foyer, which in a small way may have contributed to the difficulties between the seller and the buyer. The first view, or first impression, inside a home holds a prominent place in feng shui. Here, the bathroom door opens directly across from the front door. Part of the first impression of this stately home, therefore, is the bright, shiny silver plumbing under the bathroom sink. The reflection of light off the plumbing immediately grabs my attention

The first impression of this home includes the bathroom that is situated directly across from the front door. Feng shui adjustments include a large plant, a mirror, and a skirt under the sink.

(chi). As chi enters the home, much of it exits down these exposed pipes. Bathrooms have the largest drains in the home, and when a bathroom is directly across from the entrance, chi energy tends to enter the home only to take the shortest route out, literally going "down the drain," instead of circulating through the living spaces. Another helpful solution is to keep a cover or plug over the drain.

There are three methods to counter this situation: (1) conceal the pipes, and (2) place a mirror on the bathroom wall to send some of the chi energy back into the foyer. Pipes may be concealed with a sink skirt or built-in cabinets; these are attractive solutions that provide a bit of extra storage space. Other options include a short folding screen of paper, wood, or fabric, or a basket of tall silk flowers or silk greenery fanning out in front of the pipes. (3) Keep the bathroom door closed and hang a mirror on the outside of the door.

Exposed plumbing has the potential to be draining and devastating for one's financial resources. Whenever a building has exposed pipes for plumbing, especially those that carry water out of the building, it is wise to conceal them. Water has many connections to money in the East, and ideally one should not be able to see the exit route for the water. Exposed plumbing never looks very attractive, so for beauty's sake alone this is a worthwhile alteration. But, it will have its payoff in terms of chi as well.

A Welcoming Foyer

In the foyer, a tall palm plant intercepts some of the chi energy before it enters the bathroom. This helps accumulate chi in the foyer and creates an uplifting, nurturing feeling as soon as you enter the home. Fortunately, the foyer is generously sized, so the proximity of the bathroom to the entrance is not a problem. The foyer's size, combined with abundant natural lighting, creates a welcoming, supportive environment—a desirable first impression. Beautiful decorative items hint at the artistic and spiritual interests of the family, and aesthetic beauty and spiritual objects speak to the soul.

Orientation Adjustment

This home's front door faces 310 degrees northwest, not the best direction for any family member. The pa-kua system of feng shui uses the compass to align individuals and the specific energetic quality of an orientation. (See chapter 11 for more on fortunate directions.) Mirrors carefully placed can pull images of the front door to the east and west, thereby covering the best directions of each family member.

Door placement is a bit unusual here, as the "front" door is on what appears to be the side of the home. The backyard resides to the left of the front door, not at the true rear of the home. What appears to be the front of the home—the side that faces the road—has only windows, no entrance. Nonetheless, the ba-gua is oriented to the main door.

Because the facing direction of this home is northwest, the center of the opposite wall, or the *sitting direction,* faces southeast. The overall essence of the home is thus categorized under the Wood element, as southeast and east are the two directions governed by the Wood element. The overall energy of the home, in this case the Wood element, is compared to the natal element of each family member. Control cycles are adjusted as necessary to create balance and harmony.

Diverting Negative Energy

While assessing the area surrounding the home, I notice another house farther down the hill that is diagonal to this one, sending a line of sha—negative, unbalanced energy—directly toward a window in the living room. Nature seldom moves or grows in straight lines: Rivers turn and bend, trees branch out. Sha, on the other hand, travels in straight lines and may be transmitted along straight rows of trees, angled-corner edges of rooftops, heavy utility wires, or a road or bridge pointing at one's home; it can be deflected in a number of ways. At the point where the sha enters Jane's home, there is visible evidence of decay. The window has leaked for quite some time. While it is best to have no direct lines of sha pointing toward your home, it is even more important to have no sha directed

Before:

Peter's desk sat in a "rushing river of chi" caused by the five side-by-side windows. This position also placed his back toward the entrance. Though this placement is not as problematic in a home office as it would be in an office building, it is not ideal.

After:

Now with a solid backing behind it, the placement of Peter's desk provides a wide view of his entire office from a command position.

toward a door or window, especially bedroom windows. We are at our most vulnerable when we are asleep, at which time we require an especially calm surrounding of chi.

To intercept and disperse the straight-line energy directed at this property, there are many possible feng shui cures: Peter and Jane could install a tall fence, evergreen shrubs or trees, a fountain, a ba-gua mirror hung on the inside or the outside of the home to reflect back the sha, a hanging plant, or even wind chimes hung outside the living room window.

Creating a Functional Office

The home office, used almost exclusively by Peter, poses several challenges. Peter feels somewhat stuck in his career and would like to see some changes; he is also not as productive as he would like to be. These concerns do not surprise me when I notice the placement of Peter's desk. It is not in a command position—one that provides a full view of the room, including its entrance, and places a solid wall at one's back. Peter's back is to the entrance. Even worse, the desk is centered in a bay window, in the middle of a torrent of chi. Rearranging the furniture according to Peter's personal best directions improved things considerably.

Linear Forms

Forms made up of straight lines meeting at right angles could not be more opposite to the forms of the natural world; they are, for better or worse, man-made forms. Straight lines with their insensitive, imposed, and alien nature obstruct and destroy this harmonious, life-giving force.
–Christopher Day (Places of the Soul)

Originally, Peter's desk faced southwest, his absolute worst direction. Using information from the pa-kua school (see chapter 11), Peter's desk was placed to face his best direction, southeast, and he can now see who enters his office, which brings him a new level of comfort and relaxation. No doubt, he will be more productive in this arrangement.

Placing plants in the bay window to redirect chi helps modify the chi in the office. Both the look and feel of the room are more pleasing after these minor adjustments. Once a room has undergone transformation with feng shui, a deeper understanding emerges: We realize that we've found exactly what we've been looking for.

Small Changes Make All the Difference

In the kitchen, the cabinets do not reach the ceiling, a common feature in many homes. The space between the top of the cabinets and the ceiling traps chi. This can be easily remedied with silk greenery, a low maintenance reminder of nature that is especially helpful in a hard-to-reach area.

Off the kitchen, the breakfast room houses Jane's stereo, chaise, and desk. She has never been happy with this room and does not use it as often as she once thought she might. One possible reason might be the fact that the room sits entirely outside of the geometric shape of the house: It is isolated—not part of the main body of the home. While the added structure of the breakfast room increases the ability of the home to support Family/Health, adjustments are needed to move the energy around the room and integrate it into the rest of the home. To remedy this, we place a mirror on the room's southeast wall, visually circulating some of the room's energy into the Wealth corner of the home. To elevate the feeling of wholeness in the home and to energetically "square off" the architecture, an assortment of shrubbery and trees is planted on either side of the breakfast room in both the General Knowledge/Wisdom area (lower-left corner) and the Wealth area (upper-right corner).

As was done in the home office for Peter, we move Jane's desk so it faces one of her best directions. We also angle her chaise in a corner so it faces another beneficial direction. Above the desk is a large western-facing window. When the sun sets, it creates a lot of glare and brings glints of sha. A crystal hung in the window fills the space with beautiful bands of color, recirculating the sun's powerful chi energy. This rainbow lighting quality is classified under the Earth element, which makes it quite pleasing to Jane as this is her natal element. To further filter some of the light and glare, plants are added to the window area.

In the lounge, the room where the family spends most of its time, a chair sits by itself in a bay window, flooded by rushing chi. Seldom does anyone use this isolated chair. To remedy this, we place a table in front of the bay window and angle the chair in a corner, making it part of a comfortable conversational grouping. A plant on the table moderates the flow of chi.

Bay windows are desirable architectural elements because they replicate part of the auspicious shape of the octagon. However, the projecting corners that frame a bay window cut sharply into a room. Hard, projecting edges in architecture pierce into the smooth, spiraling movement of chi. To soften such edges, we use floor plants and hanging plants to obscure the corners with the organic shapes of nature.

Fire in the Bedroom

The master bedroom, located in the southern corner of the home, falls under the Fire element, a fabulous placement for Jane and Peter, as Fire is the nourishing element for their natal Earth elements. A mirror hangs on the wall behind their bed, not a desirable placement in feng shui not only because mirrors are among the most powerful ways to move chi in a room (too powerful and active to sleep under), but also due to the Chinese view that the soul exits the body at night and it should not be reflected in a mirror facing the foot or head of the bed. To remedy this, Jane replaces the mirror with a lovely painting of a Japanese teapot and eight oranges. It brings happiness and good energy to the bedroom.

Healing Placement

After learning the most favorable directions for her sons, Jane moved Ben, Chris, and Tom to different bedrooms, making use of the best possible furniture

arrangement for each son. Chris was a particular concern, as we hoped to give him support to help his chronic ear problems. Because Chris was born under the Wood element, he was moved to a room in the home's northern corner, which is ruled by his nourishing element Water. Because the Water element governs the ears, it is possible this change will support healing.

Moving Chi Adds Excitement

Before (top):
An isolated chair sits in front of a bank of five windows. The rust on the left window is where sha used to hit the home before intercepting wind chimes were hung.

After (above):
The brown velvet chair is no longer isolated. Closed draperies on the right provide a backdrop for the angled armchair. Greenery softens edges that project into the room and would move chi out of the alcove. The television, angled in the Wealth area, helps keep energy moving in that area.

All the feng shui adjustments discussed here were done one day when the children were at school. On arriving home, Ben, Tom, and Chris started jumping around. Ben, then thirteen years old, said, "When I walked in, something hit me and I felt too tall." His aura— the subtle electromagnetic field surrounding each of us—felt the dramatic change in the energy of his home. Children often act from an instinctual level, not editing their thoughts and feelings. In their natural innocence, they are quite open to and affected by chi energy. A chi-balanced home can go a long way in supporting a child's well-being and, at the same time, can bring a gentle, secure, calming influence to their lives.

Jane finds the changes in her house and life to be "absolutely staggering!" Within one month, Peter began a consulting firm, a longtime dream he had entertained for many years. Jane has more clarity about her desires, strengths, and motivations and is following her own dream of starting a health center that emphasizes natural therapies. And their house really feels like a home filled with warmth, happiness, and enthusiasm.

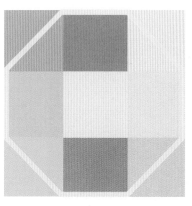

Cape Cod–Style Home Phoenix, Maryland

Harmony in our surroundings is no mere luxury. Our surroundings are the framework which subtly confine, organize and color our daily lives.
—Christopher Day, *Artist and Sculptor*

A triangular plot (which would be governed by the Fire element) signals difficulty for the inhabitants of this home. Constant disputes with neighbors and three lightning strikes on the property suggest dynamic, unbalanced energy. When not balanced with feng shui, triangular plots are too unstable and active to support harmonious living. The home's original green door (Wood element) fed the Fire element to the point of discomfort. With feng shui, the home can become much more comfortable and appealing.

Home History and Hopes

Suzanne and Phil have lived in this home for almost four years. Suzanne feels something is not quite right about the home but can't put her finger on it. She feels very boxed in, and she can't seem to finish redecorating the bedroom.

According to Suzanne, the previous owners must have thought they were building their dream home. They expected they would live happily in the home for the rest of their lives, but the wife tired of the husband. Eventually, she lived upstairs, and he lived downstairs. Alcohol was a problem, and a friend of Suzanne feels there is a lot of negative energy trapped in the staircase, where arguing and yelling likely took place between the first and second floors. Removing this residual chi with feng shui cures clears the home for the new owners.

Front entrance
The green door looks nice, but its
Wood energy only fuels the home's
excessive Fire.

Suzanne is most interested in using feng shui to unleash her creativity and to find an appropriate outlet for her creative energies. She wants to explore her creative side—to sing, dance, act, and write. Feng shui can enhance and direct creative energies and is a grounding force for strength, balance, and inspiration.

As Within, So Without

Suzanne feels that there is much movement in her life at this time. She believes she has changed rapidly during the last eight years, and she wishes her home would change with her. She wants to improve the look and energy of her home, so that it will better represent who she is. Because the principal goal of our souls is to grow and to deepen in the awareness of our own connection to the spirit in all of life, I ask Suzanne to consider her deepest sense of inner being and how she wants her home to reflect this. Consistent with her hope for a more formal floor plan, Suzanne envisions classic styling, with columns and flowing draperies. She believes that, in this setting, she might feel supported to deepen her understanding of the mysteries of life and connect with a deeper truth and knowledge.

Suzanne and Phil searched for a home for months before finding this one. Interestingly, they felt just "all right" about this Cape Cod–style home when they saw it, but the three-and-one-half-acre property is what they loved. Feng shui always considers the relativity between different components of a design. The existing galley kitchen is totally out of proportion with the rest of the house. Because the home was built according to the previous owners' plans, the small kitchen might indicate there was little nourishing energy in their lives.

Suzanne did not like the country-cottage style of the decor when they bought the home, and she looked forward to redecorating it to reflect her own tastes. Years later, even though she has redecorated, Suzanne seldom entertains and still doesn't feel happy in her home. She doesn't even want people to come to visit. Because her own cosmetic changes to the home don't please Suzanne, it seems the problem is more elemental. With prodding, Suzanne admits she doesn't like the casual design of her home. She wants a more formal plan, one that includes a sense of timelessness and antiquity. In addition, she doesn't like the narrow staircase, wants a bedroom/home office on the second floor, and wants to change the occasionally too-open feel of the great room on the first floor.

Protecting the Back of the Home

Glass spans the back of the kitchen and dining room because the home is designed to be passive solar. Large expanses of glass "leak" chi, and this particular design leaves the back of the home open and exposed. Added evergreens will provide a protective shield to the rear of the house. Additional interior "cures," especially in the kitchen, will mediate and balance the chi for the home.

Drawing the Line with Neighbors

As I turned off the main road into the shared driveway, I saw a huge pile of rubble. Large pieces of concrete were being excavated from the neighboring property.

Formerly, Suzanne and Phil's land was owned by the neighbor. At some level, it seems, the neighbor feels that all of the property is still his. Boundary disputes and other unpleasantries occur regularly, and it is unfortunate that Suzanne and Phil must share their drive with such an unneighborly neighbor. To remedy this, a pair of "guardians"—in the form of statues, trees, or columns—will be placed at the fork to their portion of the driveway and on their doorstep.

Considering the list of plants and trees and their symbolism (see chapter 11), I recommend that juniper trees or shrubs be planted in a multiple of nine, a most auspicious number for wholeness and completion. The juniper tree represents protection, and when planted along the edge of the property in a meandering line, they will augment healthy boundaries for this parcel of land and its owners.

The land itself is shaped like a triangle, one of the most unfortunate shapes for property. Energy on property with a triangular shape can be abrupt and hazardous. To balance this intensity, an evergreen might be planted in the apex of the triangle. For this particular site, an evergreen and more juniper will be helpful. The juniper's protective symbolism, coupled with its free-form shape (Water element), will help control the Fire energy of the triangular plot.

Inviting More Chi

To direct more chi into a home, the front door must be used. Simply because of its larger size and central location in this home, the spacious foyer will accumulate and distribute chi more evenly than the small side entrance, which leads into the laundry room and traps chi. Interestingly, the side door is located in the Helpful People area of the ba-gua. Because the side entrance dead-ends directly into the laundry room, it is not particularly inviting for Helpful People chi. To remedy this, a pair of louvered swinging doors or a beautiful fabric curtain, slightly gathered to one side, can assist the circulation of chi through the rest of the house.

The color red, which consists of slower and larger wavelengths, helps to attract chi (and people!) to the appropriate entrance. The shade of red does not matter, but it should be a red you really love. Use feng shui as your guidepost, then follow your intuition by paying attention to what moves you deeply.

Cooling the Fire

Since this front door faces 355 degrees north (Water element), the center of the back of the house—the "sitting" position—is south (Fire element). The home's overall energy comes from the Fire element. This, coupled with the property's triangular shape, has no doubt caused problems. Following are some anecdotes about this home that illustrate how harmful one element, when out of balance, can be.

Lightning Does Strike Twice

In the short time that Suzanne and Phil have lived here, lightning has struck the front yard on three separate occasions. In the first incident, lightning hit the cable TV line located in the Wisdom/General Knowledge area of the property. Next, lightning hit the well head, which is located in the Helpful People/Travel area. Most recently, lightning hit a tree located in the Career/Life Journey area. It's quite possible that the intense Fire energy of the property and home—remember, it's passive solar!—is attracting more Fire energy.

On the exterior, the Fire element appears yang, but the inner quality of its energy is the opposite, yin. We must strive, in our homes and in our bodies, to achieve a balance of yin/yang and the five elements and to find equilibrium.

Darkness and Light

The home has a predominantly dark quality, which is surprising, given the fact that it's a solar house. On first thought, this seems beneficial, because dark is yin and it can potentially balance the yang Fire. On deeper reflection, however, it becomes clear that while the Fire energy has a large yang exterior, it must have an equally large yin interior. A universal law of energy states, "The bigger the front, the bigger the back." Therefore, the unbalanced darkness of the home (yin) cannot possibly create an equilibrium given the more extensive imbalance. To remedy this, adding lighting and brighter colors (both yang elements) will foster the realization of the Tao of energy, a balance of yin/yang. Balanced energy in our outer environment nurtures a state of balance in our inner selves and vice versa: As we feel greater inner equilibrium, we wish to bring more harmony to our environment.

Other Strange Happenings and Coincidences

Fire energy abounds in this home. In the hallway leading from the side door to the laundry room, a fire extinguisher was stored in the closet. One day it exploded, blowing a hole in the ceiling. The neighbor and the negative chi left from the previous owners produce an aura of anger (Wood, which nourishes Fire). In addition, the previous owners used tobacco and alcohol, which are both ruled by Fire. (For more information on the elements governing foods, consult the research by Dr. Jack Garvey, which is shared in the writings of Anne Marie Colbin.)

Fighting Fire with Fire

Feng shui seldom treats homeopathically (i.e., like treating like). The usual process brings about balance through the other elements. In an extreme case such as this, however, the red (Fire element) on the door might be considered a homeopathic remedy. Just as fires are sometimes set purposely to create boundaries for forest fires that are raging out of control, our intention here (a most important aspect of feng shui) is for the red on the door to repel much of the Fire energy of the surrounding site while, at the same time, attracting more chi to the home.

Fire controls Suzanne's natal Metal element. When a balanced Fire element meets a Metal element, it can forge the Metal into something beautiful and powerful, strengthening its quality. Blacksmiths use fire to form gorgeous wrought-iron ware. Cutlery companies and sword makers use fire to strengthen and hone blades. Only when the Fire element rages out of control, overwhelming the Metal element, does a meltdown occur.

Unlike Suzanne, Phil is at ease in this home. Being born under the Fire ele-

A mirror, lighting, artwork, and plants augment the Career area of Phil and Suzanne's living room. One plant is positioned to soften the projecting corner of the built-in bookcase. Black, the color representing the Career area, is beautifully displayed in the lacquered console.

ment, he can thrive here. To help create "energetic room" for Suzanne, the Water element, which controls Fire, must flow through part of the home. A fountain in the foyer will be a wonderful source of moving water.

A River (of Chi) Runs Through It

Starting at the front door, there is a direct path of chi that travels through the living room entrance, the patio entrance, and out the back door. The fountain will help pool some chi in the foyer, but additional adjustments are needed to redistribute the chi before its exit. Visual focal points in the foyer will ground and accumulate chi for distribution throughout the home. A crystal hanging in the path of chi might help somewhat, but a stronger visual step would have a greater impact. A mural painted on the wall, perhaps a scene reminiscent of a Greek temple, would bring a touch of Suzanne's heartfelt wish for a more classical design to the entrance of her home. To recirculate chi, a crystal hangs in the doorway leading to the patio and a ba-gua mirror acts as the final guardian of chi, hanging on the door frame above the back door, the mirrored side facing into her home.

Cooking with Chi

Suzanne and I imagined the ba-gua over her house and proceeded to the Romantic Relationship/Marriage corner, located in the kitchen. Here, Suzanne said, she feels she's in a whirlwind of energy. Again, we find the persuasive Fire element represented by the stove in an angled island at the center of the kitchen. The Fire energy in this home is active, assertive, aggressive. Most of the surfaces in the kitchen are highly glossy and reflective (e.g., glass, slick Formica countertops, and glazed ceramic flooring), characteristics of the Water element that do help to control some of the excessive Fire element, but not completely. The Earth element can also diffuse some of the Fire element's strength. Because Fire nourishes Earth, Earth necessarily reduces some of Fire's force. A collection of earthenware—a terra-cotta pedestal and ceramic serving bowls and planters—now brings more Earth element to the kitchen, which reduces some of the excess Fire element. Suzanne benefits additionally, since Earth is her nourishing element.

Phil and Suzanne's marriage relationship is augmented by the expansion and beauty created by their recent renovation of the kitchen, which is located in the Relationship area of the home.

Our Surroundings Affect the Way We Think, Feel, and Work

At one side of the kitchen is an area where Suzanne spends a fair amount of time paying bills and making phone calls. She is not pleased with the way this space looks or functions. It's the dumping spot for all the mail and packages. It doesn't take long for the area to look cluttered, which really bothers Suzanne. On first glance, it seemed a professional organizer might be needed. But just under the counter area are four drawers that should certainly be able to support the organization of the mail. Many items presently in the drawers can be stored in other areas of the home. Simply reorganizing a few things gives Suzanne a lot more room where she needs it most.

Because Suzanne sits in this area, it should be special for her. I suggest adding lots of texture, which will incorporate her nourishing Earth element and will also balance many of the slick, shiny surfaces. Artwork and special objects with an ancient Grecian look and feel will create the sense of ages past that Suzanne loves.

This area falls under the Children/Creative Projects area of the ba-gua. Because enhancing her creativity is Suzanne's principal goal and focus at this point in her life, we make feng shui adjustments to ground her creative energy. A tall modern glass vase sits in the window near Suzanne's desk, and beautiful pens and colorful notepads await her ideas. The height of the vase is significant, as the Wood element's shape is vertical and it governs creativity. A plant graces the counter alongside her desk; energetically, a plant encourages growth in the area of the ba-gua in which it is placed. Together, the plant (Wood element) and the white color (for Children/Creativity located here, on the middle right side, of her home) enhance consciousness and awareness. Finally, personal mementos from previous musical performances and notices of upcoming musical events forge a strong connection to the creative musical energy Suzanne wants to create in her life.

Every object in our homes has the potential to reveal and support those aspects of our lives that we most wish to create. Possibility abounds with feng shui.

The Earth Element Governs Nourishment

The dining room falls under the Metal element and, interestingly, all of the furniture in the dining room is made of brass and glass. Brass is governed by both Metal and Earth elements because of its material and color, respectively; glass, ruled by the Water element, is reflective. A lovely medium tone of purple covers the walls. Purple, related to the color red, carries a lot of Fire energy; however, darker and bluer shades represent Water. (See chapter 2 for additional element and color information.)

Because the Earth element nourishes the northwest Metal element dining room, Suzanne is considering using a salmon color on the walls. This room diminishes Phil's Fire element because his natal Fire controls the room's Metal. At the same time, the green (Wood element) fabric on the dining room chairs brings in a nourishing touch for Phil. All five elements are represented in this room.

The ceiling in the dining room slants and creates a waterfall of rushing chi in the room. Mirrored pedestals holding cascading plants and sculptures are placed carefully below the lower end of the ceiling, serving as sentinels to balance the movement of chi. In order to nourish Suzanne's natal element and the room's Metal elements, heavy texture (Earth element) should be used in objects. A highly textured ceramic bowl (Earth element) for the center of the dining room table and a buffet table or serving piece cultivate support for entertaining and formal dinners.

Possible window treatments should combine the two sides of Suzanne's personality: her formal classical side and free-spirited, artistic side. A brass curtain rod will repeat the elegant style of the dining room table, but an organic form, such as a tree branch or a length of bamboo, will subtly strengthen both of their nourishing elements—Wood and Earth—in form and color.

Wealth Corner in the Living Room

In the far left corner of the living room, the Wealth area of the ba-gua, there is a beautiful mirrored folding screen in a contemporary design. Tucked back into a corner between two windows, the screen sends beautiful, sparkling light around the living room. Because no one sits directly across from this screen, no one's image is broken by the small widths of mirror. Feng shui is a process of viewing ourselves as whole in body, mind, and spirit, which is not supported by images broken up by mirror fragments. A very small decorative mirror, less than four inches in size, works as a cure, since a mirror that small is not used for viewing oneself.

Mirrors should not cut the image of the top, bottom, or sides of one's face. There is even a physical connection: The result could be headaches. Any mirror should reflect the entire head of an adult living in the home. It should be low enough for a shorter person to use as well as high enough for the tallest family member to see his or her head reflected fully. The head is the main concern for viewing in mirrors. Children primarily use bathroom mirrors, so be sure these reflect each child's entire head.

A mirror in the Wealth corner should not be large because it can symbolize a portal, allowing wealth to slip out of the house.

On the opposite side of the living room, the Helpful People/Travel ninth, a corner is missing, which no doubt contributes to some of this home's unfortunate energy. A tall floor plant, backlit with a can light placed on the floor and angled toward the corner, softens the harsh edge, increases the energy, and moves chi around this corner. Enhancing the Fame/Advancement portion in the back center third of their home, a floor lamp sits next to a mirrored pedestal that holds a fabulous arrangement of exquisite silk flowers that was designed by Phil as a gift to Suzanne. Its realistic colors and shapes are pleasant reminders of both the beauty of flowers at their peak and the healing powers of nature.

A mirrored folding screen, plants, lighting, and flowers amplify energy in the Wealth area.

Tones of Colors Combine Elements

The master bedroom is ruled by the Earth element, Suzanne's nourishing element. Burgundy is a wonderful color for bedding and window treatments, as it brings together the room's nourishing element and Phil's natal Fire element, which is tempered by the Water element (black) so it is not too much fire for Suzanne. The light oak bedroom furniture stands out in delightful contrast

Live plants or silk greenery above bulkheads and over window areas provide a graceful path for chi to follow.

against the dark tones. Two mirrors over the dresser create a large reflective surface and are too activating to chi for the bedroom. To remedy this, a piece of artwork will replace one of the mirrors, creating an asymmetrical arrangement.

Try as she might, for three years Suzanne has not been able to finish decorating the master bedroom. With feng shui as her guide, however, many design decisions are falling into place. New draperies, bed skirt, duvet, and a medium tone on the walls will enhance relaxation time spent in the bedroom and will support the marital relationship with a new level of beauty and comfort.

Moving Chi, Even in the Bathroom

In the master bathroom, a skylight over the bathtub brightens the room. Adding a crystal or a hanging plant in the window well moves chi and enhances the room even more. The rainbow light patterns created by a crystal fall within the Earth element. To lighten the feel of the overhead bulkhead, greenery reaches down over the edge and is enhanced by recessed lighting. A swag of silk greenery and flowers graces the top of the bathroom window, adding visual interest to the narrow wall. Mirrored closet doors face the mirrored wall behind the vanity to create an intriguing interplay of reflections.

Clearing Rituals

The stairwell, site of residual arguing energy, must be cleared of unwanted negative chi. Because the former owners lived much of their lives on separate floors in this home, the stairway was the de facto entrance to the wife's living space. Firecrackers use intense soundwaves to blast away old chi. One or nine firecrackers are used as clearing tools, depending on intuition, the degree of need, and the location. In this home, we use one firecracker augmented by prayer and visualizations to clear the chi of this space.

Room for Chi to Move

On the second floor, there are two guest bedrooms and a crowded multipurpose room. Almost every square foot of the latter is occupied. It contains a twin bed, a chair, two tables, a television, a desk, and storage units, among other things. Rarely does Suzanne use this room for its intended purpose of sewing and writing. The room feels claustrophobic, and its energy feels stagnant and stifled. The room's many objects ground and hold chi, leaving little room for flow. To create a balance of open space allowing for the free movement of chi, storage pieces holding nonessential items are moved to the basement. In addition, we removed one seldom-used table and turned the twin bed into a settee, eliminating the need for a lounge chair. With more open space, the energy moves in a more harmonious way.

An Ongoing Process

Because not all feng shui cures are immediate, it is best to create a list of what you need for each room of your home. Carry it with you, and keep your eyes open for possible solutions when you are on vacation or browsing through catalogues. You will be amazed how the right cures have a way of finding you. Once you know what types of things you are looking for, synchronicity quite often moves in to support the process.

Delighted with all of the recommendations for their home, Suzanne and Phil are amazed at the many levels addressed by feng shui. There is the psychological level, the energetic level, and the decorative level. Being sensitive and receptive to all three brings balance, harmony, and beauty to our lives.

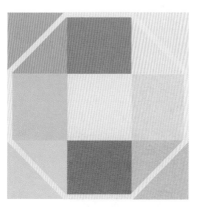

Converted Barn
Butler, Maryland

Earthly things must be known to be loved: divine things must be loved to be known.
—Blaise Pascal, *Mathematician and Philosopher*

This might be the most unique home I've ever visited. A converted barn, the home is filled with beautiful, earthy, handcrafted objects, and its exterior is embellished with many natural, interesting finds. The owners, Stanford and Theresa, collect Native American art and artifacts.

Overall, they are very happy with their home. Since they consider their connection to nature and their spiritual development to be of paramount importance in their lives, they wish to explore any insights the ancient wisdom of feng shui may offer.

Intuitively following feng shui gardening precepts, Stanford has created beautiful landscaping—curving beds of evergreens and flowers surround the home.

On many levels, this home represents the Earth element—from its large rectangular shape to the exterior colors. Even the compass directions reflect this element. One immediately feels this grounding and stability when approaching this home. In just one year, they planted more than two thousand tulips and nearly two hundred azaleas. The undulating landscape, large crystals, and sculpture tap and pool chi from the earth. The feeling and energy on this land are sublime and uniquely delicate.

At one time all seventy acres of this property was underwater; the land is mineral rich and lush. The home sits near the bottom of a valley, located in what was once a floodplain. At one time, a major river ran through this land, but a dam and drainage construction diverted most of the water, allowing for home sites. Many of the nearby rivers have dried up to smaller streams. A gentle, meandering stream passes directly in front of this home, foretelling of abundant chi and constant opportunities. In one of the most beautiful examples of the "pooling" of chi I've ever seen, two rivers converge just west of the home, flowing eastward into a beautiful pond in front of the home. The pond is stocked with fish, symbols of success.

When two rivers join together and flow directly in front of this home, a powerful force results, which brings to Stanford and Theresa a flow of chi, bountiful health, and many opportunities.

Touch the Earth

It is easy to see how flowing and grounded chi—the streams and the pond, respectively—supports Stanford and Theresa's lives. Their retail business, a music, book, and gift shop, has grown dramatically. Never actively seeking opportunities, opportunities continue to find Stanford and Theresa. They are beginning a wholesale business and have moved to a new downtown location, doubling the size of their previous store.

Both born in the Year of the Ox at around 6 P.M., Stanford and Theresa have an ascendant ruled by the rooster. Our ascendant is our outward demeanor—the way we appear to others. It also colors the way we see the world. Stanford and Theresa's shared rooster ascendant speaks to a joint pioneering spirit in a quest for knowledge. Theresa's birth year was ruled by yin energy, under the Metal element: a Yin Metal Ox year. Because Metal governs the year of Theresa's birth, she innately has strong monetary instincts and clear convictions, both of which compel her to business success. Stanford's birth year was also ruled by yin energy, under the Fire element: a Yin Fire Ox year. The Fire energy ruling Stanford's birth year makes him a natural leader, decisive and sure of himself. The ox is a steady worker that is determined to persevere for the common good. Those born in the Year of the Ox are also ruled by Water (see chapter 11), so Stanford and Theresa's personalities are fed and enhanced by the water on their property.

It is interesting that two people born in the Year of the Ox chose a converted barn for their home. The transformation of this barn into a home is really stunning. The home site is unique and sacred, full of favorite, symbolic pieces, which help augment some of the weak chi of this residence. Because the space was originally designed as a barn, the home chi is weak. On some basic level, the original intentions of the owner, architect, and builder remain part of a space, almost like the karma of a structure. However, with careful adjustments, intention can be transformed. Here, special belongings (one of the nine categories of feng shui adjustments) work to elevate chi. The power lies more in your connection to an item than in the item itself. Favorite belongings, especially those of a sacred nature, or belongings with an emotional relevance may be used in any area of the ba-gua for your spirit's connection, intention, and inspiration.

Facing Position/Sitting Position

The home faces southwest, the Earth element. The back of the home, the sitting position, faces northeast. Because the northeast also falls under the Earth element, the home abounds with Earth energy. While this is wonderful for Stanford, who was born under the Earth element, it is too much for Theresa who was born under the Wood element (Wood controls Earth and is reduced by it).

Providing an overall remedy for Theresa involves increasing the Wood element in the home. Lots of plants; the colors blue, green, and teal; and items with tall, columnar shapes will help. Wood elements lend added control for all of the Earth energy of the home. Further, the Metal element, through the colors white and silver or metal items might also be used to balance the home's energy for Theresa, as Metal reduces Earth energy. Metal energy must be used sparingly, however, as it is the controlling element for Theresa's Wood.

Within the Five Element Theory are deeper levels and intricacies. Each element has a big and a small category (i.e., big wood, small wood, etc.). Within these intricacies there are always beneficial aspects to the control and reduction cycles. The reduction cycle results from the control cycle; whenever an element controls another, it is reduced in the process. Here, though Earth reduces Wood (because Wood is the control of Earth), it also provides a firm, stable place for Theresa's natal Wood element to send down deep roots, allowing her Wood energy to ground, flourish, and expand.

Directing the Energetic "Traffic"

On entering this home, you are greeted by a wonderful open feeling created mainly by light from a large window across from the door and the home's two-story foyer. Unfortunately, while the home's design makes the space feel expansive, it also pulls a lot of chi up to the second floor before it circulates through the first. This imbalance is amplified by the stairway's location directly across from the entrance. If the stairs were more than twelve feet away from the entrance, this would be less of a problem. However, because the stairs are less than twelve feet from the door, a cure is needed to ground chi on the first floor, before it rushes up the stairs. A crystal hanging midway between the entrance and the stairs, and suspended from the ceiling on a nine-inch length of thin wire (a fortunate number) helps capture and redistribute chi.

Because the stair risers are open, greenery placed under them will help circulate the human chi that otherwise would slip through the risers and stagnate under the stairs every time someone uses them. Also, to deter the exit of chi from the front door to the large window opposite, a beautiful stained-glass window hangs in the upper pane.

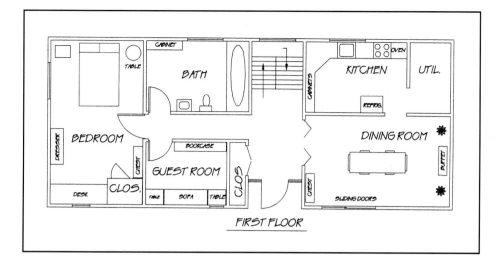

FIRST FLOOR

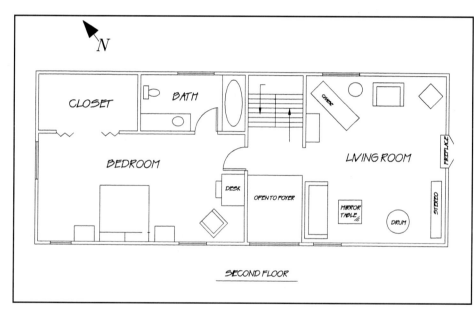

SECOND FLOOR

The Ming Tang or center of the home is pleasantly open and uncluttered. Air circulates easily, an important factor for the movement of chi. In the foyer, a statue of Kwan Yin, the goddess of compassion, sits on a table, one of the many sacred and meaningful objects found throughout the home. Because Kwan Yin's presence greets the visitor, compassion enhances the quality of energy entering the home.

Tracing the Nine-Star Path

Laying the ba-gua over the entire first floor, we trace the nine-star path, considering each area of the ba-gua as it relates to Stanford and Theresa's goals. Symbolic colors or items are placed in any area of the ba-gua one wishes to highlight. These items bring light, beauty, color, and suggestions of nature to our surroundings. As visual reminders, they support our goals and openness in life. Many items seem practical and are based on common sense; others may seem illogical or mystical—both work!

The Three Transcendental Cures

When administering any feng shui cure, or when you wish to use an item already in place in an area of the ba-gua, you can make the adjustment even more effective by performing the three transcendental cures, symbolic gestures that bring

Kwan Yin, the goddess of compassion, stands in the foyer. This special statue, which inspires Theresa and Stanford, is one among many pieces that augment the spiritual quality of this home.

power to your process of feng shui. In *Living Color*, Professor Lin Yun, in a very charming manner, describes this level of feng shui as holding 140 percent of the effectiveness, whereas all of the physical items and adjustments we make may hold only 20 to 40 percent of the effectiveness. This comparison illustrates the immense importance of the three transcendental cures. Remember, during this ritual it is important to keep the chi moving in your body by breathing fully and slowly. The origin of the word *spirit* is the Latin verb *spirare,* which means "to breathe."

First Cure

Clear the space energetically with either a wave of your hands, a physical cleaning (which also involves a wave of your hand), or the traditional Tibetan Buddhist method of a *mudra*, a hand position. This "ousting mudra" represents the clearing of negativity, past, present, and future. You form a circle with your two middle fingers and your thumbs while keeping your index fingers and little fingers relatively straight. You then flick your two middle fingers outward and upward nine times. You may use both hands, or a female will use her right hand, a male his left.

Second Cure

Say one line of a prayer, sing one line of a song, or say the following chant nine times: OM MANI PADME HUM (om ma-nee pod-may hum). This chant is a prayer to the feminine aspect of God asking for peace, prosperity, and compassion. It is through the repetition of the single line that you move your mind to a meditative, open, receptive place, aligning body, mind, and spirit.

Third Cure

Work with creative visualization. The more visually specific you can be on the theater screen of your mind's eye, the better. The right side of the brain plays an important role in the attraction and creation of deeper levels and new aspects of life. If you can conceive, you can achieve. Open yourself to intuition and nonlinear thought. Then conceive many creative visual scenes as you focus on what you would like to create in an area of the ba-gua you choose to enhance with feng shui.

The Ba-gua Matrix

A matrix is something that gives origin or form to another thing. The following matrix refers specifically to the first floor of Stanford and Theresa's home. "Walking" through the numeric sequence—called "tracing the nine stars"—in their home will provide an example for you to follow in your own.

Position 1 (middle-left ninth): Family/Health. In this home, position 1 falls in the middle of the downstairs bedroom. A mirror and a collection of antique colored-glass bottles bring beauty and movement, through the reflection of light, to this area. A beam spans the ceiling here, but a mobile of a flying angel breaks the straight line of the beam and moves chi around the protrusion, which would have been more problematic had it resided directly over the bed.

Position 2 (upper-left ninth): Wealth. Position 2 is located in the upper portion of the bedroom. Here, artwork in red, blue, and purple amplifies the room's energy, creating vitality. There are also a few antique purses here, each holding "seed money" to grow into or attract more wealth. This seed money is wrapped in red paper or in a little red envelope, as red signifies joy. Following the cardinal rule of 50 percent undecorated space, the other two walls of this room have little decoration, providing a peaceful, open, Zen balance to this room.

The door into the bedroom is not in a direct line with the foot or side of the bed, thereby creating a peaceful and restful space. When the foot of a bed is directly across from the entrance to a room, it is called the "corpse" position, the worst bed position in feng shui. This is how corpses are laid out in China before they are carried off to be buried. A bed may be on the wall across from the entrance, but it should be placed to one side of the doorway. If the only possible position for a bed places its side directly in the walkway as you enter the room, hang a mobile or a crystal between the doorway and the side of the bed to divert the direct hit of chi.

Position 3 (center ninth): Ming Tang Spirit Pool. The center of the home, Ming Tang or position 3, is also referred to as the "reflecting pool." We stop here in a moment of contemplation to visualize the spiritual essence of the home nourishing Stanford and Theresa's inner essence and vice versa, their spiritual energy filling the home. Unfortunately, the toilet sits just on the edge of the center ninth, meaning some of the spiritual essence of the home is going "down the drain." But, not to worry, a cure is in place—an aromatherapy machine on the back of the toilet regularly emits a burst of fragrant flower essence. Scent brings vitality to body, mind, and spirit. This delightful reminder of the healing power of nature pervades the entire home. A plant on the back of the toilet also increases the energy in the Ming Tang.

Position 4 (lower-right ninth): Helpful People/Travel. The Helpful People/Travel position is found in the front of the dining room, where plants, flowers, lighting, and a mirror (small enough to miss diners' heads but large enough to double the image of dishes at the table) augment chi. Sometimes diners may feel uncomfortable looking at themselves during an entire meal; however, doubling the image of the dishes and food symbolizes doubling wealth.

In a home where someone is self-employed, as Stanford and Theresa are, the Helpful People area should especially be enhanced. Plants, mirrors, and artwork increase and ground chi. The rectangular dining table has an even number of chairs, something strongly preferred in feng shui. Ideally, the dining tables will comprise a full geometric shape with no angled corners, unless it is a true octagon. An even number of chairs represents balance and symbolizes that no one will be lonely.

Position 5 (middle-right ninth): Children/Creative Projects. Position 5 falls partially in the back of the dining room, the utilities room, and the kitchen. Plants (growth and creativity), a pet parrot (movement and communication), and a beautiful gold-leaf folding screen (gold represents radiance and riches, while the flowers represent wealth and the Wood element), add much to the energy of this area.

Position 6 (lower-left ninth): Wisdom/General Knowledge. We find position 6 in the front portion of the downstairs bedroom. Appropriately, some books are

Numerous items in Theresa and Stanford's home were made by hand by their friends. This metal lampshade comprises many of the owners' favorite symbols: spirals, stars, waves, and the moon.

stored here as well as plans for the future direction of Stanford and Theresa's store. Books support knowledge, wisdom, and self-cultivation, and play a large part in Stanford and Theresa's business.

Position 7 (upper-middle ninth): Fame/Advancement. This is another especially important area for self-employed people; it represents the spreading of one's personal and business reputation. Likewise, it is also important for anyone desiring advancement within a company or corporation. To make best use of this area's symbolic color, red flowers were planted in the flower box located outside the window in the Fame position (the back center of the home, opposite the entrance). The stained-glass window hanging here features Stanford and Theresa's natal element colors, in the Fame area.

Position 8 (lower-middle ninth): Career/Life Journey. The Career/Life Journey area falls where the main entrance is located, indicating that there is a lot of chi entering to support career paths. The indented entry is augmented by plants and touches of red to amplify the chi in this small "missing" area of the architecture.

Position 9 (upper-right ninth): Romantic Relationship/ Marriage. The final position supports the Romantic Relationship/Marriage area of life. Because a seldom-used door leading to the utilities room is located here, adding a mirror to the door will symbolize openness and movement in the love relationship. Future plans for this area include a screened-in porch and aviary.

Second Floor

There are three rooms on the second floor. It is not fortunate feng shui for a bathroom on the second floor to be located directly over a first-floor kitchen or bedroom or the front entrance. The chi movement of the exiting water affects the areas directly below, draining health and wealth. In this home, which is well planned, the second floor bath is directly above the first floor bath. In the master bedroom, the ceiling slopes, but the straight portion of the wall is fairly high. The bed affords a solid wood backing in one of the command positions (a position from which one has a full view of the room and the entry), which is also out of the path of the door. The dream catcher and lighting keep chi moving in this Wisdom/General Knowledge area of the home. Sleeping in this area of the bagua can enhance the wisdom in one's life, available through books, inner searching, or with a teacher. Shortly after moving here, Stanford began studying flute with a renowned musician, which has been a powerful and deeply rewarding process.

The left-rear corner of the second floor, the Wealth area, is a closet. The closet must be kept orderly. A niche above the closet contains a number of attractive items, as well as a mobile to assist chi movement in the Wealth area.

The home's living room resides on the second floor. Native American decor and plants abound. The living room doubles as a music room and contains drums and dozens of flutes. A mirrored coffee table sits between the Helpful People/Travel and Children/Creative Projects areas, amplifying the energy of both.

Mirrored furniture, such as this unique coffee table located in the Children/Creative Projects area, is a cure that brightens the space and amplifies and moves chi.

Wood/Water, Earth/Fire

I asked Theresa and Stanford how they feel about their natal and nourishing elements. Theresa, born under the Wood element and nourished by Water, works with herbal and flower essences (Wood) in her aromatherapy practice. She feels things very deeply, which is an aspect of the Water element. For fifteen years she swam daily as her main form of exercise and still loves spending time in the water, especially on vacations in tropical climates. We are often drawn instinctively to our natal and nourishing elements.

Stanford, born under the Earth element and nourished by Fire, believes the Earth is everything—the Mother who supports us all. He feels gratitude for that but admits Fire is important to him as well. The color red gives him a "charge," and he also enjoys cooking. Certainly, fire is extremely important in the preparation of daily food. Stanford also enjoys a good cigar (tobacco is the Fire element) shared with his father or friends.

The Home of the Spirit

Both Stanford and Theresa believe spiritual connection is of utmost importance in their lives. Their home is like a living mandala, an arrangement of one meaningful item after the next, either on altars, shelves, or tabletops. In feng shui, an altar should not be placed under a staircase, where the downward energy is suppressive, or outside a bathroom, where there is too much activity from exiting water, nor should it be visible from the front door, since an altar is meant to be kept private. The overhead lighting near an altar should be circular to replicate points of heavenly light. Scissors and medicines should not be kept on one's altar. Images of deities should be solid, not hollow. Fresh flowers and fruit are recommended. If you wish to have a candle or lamp on an altar, ideally use a pair of candles or lamps. Wood, stone, or concrete are the best materials for an altar, especially when created in auspicious measurements (see chapter 11).

Nourish your spirit by creating a daily morning ritual: Light a candle, burn incense, offer prayers, or meditate. At the beginning of the full moon, the moon is directly across from the sun, which results in a balance of yin/yang. An abundance of energy exists at this time and it is important to direct it in a positive way. Place treats on your altar on the day of the full moon and eat them the next day, giving thanks for the many blessings in your life.

Stanford and Theresa experience much peace on this property and believe that the harmony in their home is inspiring. And so it should be.

Contemporary Home
Santa Barbara, California

The physical universe is alive with forces of yin and yang. These forces can be formed in harmony or converge to interact vigorously so as to bear fruit for a dwelling and its occupants.
—Dr. Evelyn Lip, *Architect and Writer*

This home's stunning stucco and glass contemporary design demands your attention but does little to store chi energy, particularly calming chi. Feng shui adjustments will help redirect and pool chi, creating a harmonious feel in this striking home.

I've never visited Santa Barbara before and am intrigued to see a home perched at the edge of a citrus garden, filled with grapefruit, orange, and lime trees, as this home is. In class, Professor Lin Yun emphasizes the importance of

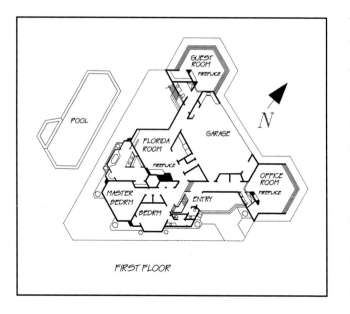

FIRST FLOOR

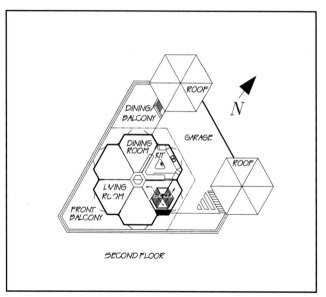

SECOND FLOOR

being aware of the many areas of life seen in subtle nuances. When attempting to understand the feng shui of a site, these are useful clues. There are many types of chi to be assessed: human chi, earth chi, heaven chi, animal chi, building chi, and weather chi. On this day, the weather chi is warm and clear, very pleasant. The flight and drive to Santa Barbara were enjoyable and direct; there were no obstacles—a good sign.

Yin/Yang Designs

The approach to this home starts at a beautifully designed iron gate, featuring curvilinear and rectilinear lines, a nice balance of forms. Curving lines represent yin, while straight lines and sharper angles represent yang. The driveway winds through a grove of fragrant trees up to this impressive stucco and glass beauty.

Heide is a writer and seminar leader who has recently developed an interest in feng shui. Her home sits halfway up a mountain, overlooking the Pacific Ocean. This huge body of water fronting her home invites wealth to her front door. Secondarily, it balances the overall shape of the home. While the main area is hexagonal—a fortunate shape, as six attracts wealth—an office addition, guest room, and garage give the home a triangular shape, which is ruled by the Fire element. Fire is too intense to dominate in the form of a building or lot. The quick-moving energy represents a hot nature. Living on a triangular property or in a similarly shaped home that isn't balanced can bring misfortune; robbery and accidents are two of the most common problems.

Assessing Needs

Heide's principal wish is to set up a supportive, appropriate work space. She also feels that there is no place in the home to "cozy up." Since moving here, Heide and

A large, faceted, leaded-glass crystal above the door, double lights, and red flowers amplify chi at the entrance to this home.

her partner have had some difficulties. They haven't always been happy, but they have been loving, and it's taken some adjustment on their part to live in this space.

The home works well for parties, but, for Heide, it seldom feels comfortable as a home should. Sensitive to energy, Heide often feels drained and uninvigorated here. She fears the house may be unmanageable because of its large size—six thousand square feet—and wonders if her need for a more inviting work space is possible here.

When addressing the feng shui needs of a home, I like to start at the front door to see where my attention is drawn or directed. Often, this visual journey follows the same pattern as chi energy as it spirals through a space.

Split Foyers, Split Chi

Imagine this entranceway: Just inside the front door, you walk into a large foyer that also serves as a landing between the upper and lower floors. To the left are stairs that go up to the living room, while straight ahead are stairs leading to a sunken Florida room. Still at the landing, facing straight ahead, there is a handrail for these stairs; the top corner of the handrail ends at about crotch height and is directly across from the entry. Energetically, this handrail functions like a karate chop each time someone enters the home; it is an example of sha, or sharp negative, unwelcome energy. To adjust this, a green vine should be grown around the handrail. Silk greenery might also be used if poor lighting conditions do not permit live plants. Tassels or a small tapestry bell pull on the edge of the handrail could work as well. By obscuring the sharp edge, Heide and her guests will feel more welcome here.

Above the handrail is an overhanging balcony that lowers the ceiling height, making the space uncomfortable on a subconscious level. From a purely visual standpoint, however, the setting and architecture are dynamic, and the furnishings are sumptuous and beautiful. Tuning into the energies of the home on a deeper level, it is clear that, on entering, there is too much going on with no real focal point to help ground chi.

Many contemporary homes today are designed with split foyers. When chi enters such a home and is immediately met by stairs going in opposite directions, it creates a feeling of chaos. The energy needs a focal point. A hanging plant in a bright, shiny planter; a leaded-glass crystal hung just above the head between the entrance and the midpoint between the two sets of stairs; or a bright piece of artwork are all possible options.

In Heide's home, a wonderful spot for a focal point is the overhang of the projecting balcony. On entering the home, this will instantly lift the eye, creating balance for the depressed energy under the balcony. Feng shui lifts our energy. When something beautiful is placed high, it catches our attention and adds interest to the area while elevating our chi.

Your Nourishing Element in Your First Impression

Because Heide was born under the Earth element, adding a touch of her nourishing Fire element to the foyer will help her feel strengthened. A bright piece of artwork that includes the color red makes an ideal feng shui adjustment for the foyer's overhanging balcony. Also, placing a tall palm tree here, an inviting touch of nature, moves chi up and along the sweeping lines of its branches, leading your eye toward the art.

The stairway to the left of the foyer, leading upstairs, has open risers. The open risers capture chi, where it can accumulate and stagnate. (When anyone uses these stairs, their energy does not remain as integrated as it would if the stairs had closed backs.) A philodendron placed under the stairs helps circulate this chi into the rest of the home. Other possible adjustments are lighting under the stairs and a leaded-glass crystal hung under and to the back of one of the stairs, located about midway between the top and bottom stair, which would help recirculate energy.

Symbolically "Moving" the Door

The wall located under the overhanging balcony is recessed. It looks dark, a sign that not much chi is present or moving. To remedy this, a mirror is hung to increase light (energy) in this area. The mirror also reflects an image of the door to one of Heide and her partner's best directions. The east-facing door (orienta-

Before (above):
The view from inside the front door. Just as your eye is drawn immediately to the back door, so is the energy.

After (right):
Several new focal points now ground energy in the foyer. A sofa table with art objects and a floor plant both function to slow the river of chi that runs through the house.

tion taken from inside the house looking out) is Heide's worst direction. However, the mirror pulls an image over to the southwest direction, as it hangs on the angled wall across from the door. The southwest is Heide's second best direction. (To learn how to locate your best directions, see chapter 11.) This directional adjustment will also help balance the entranceway's chi, redirecting it to energize other parts of the home.

Blocking the Exit of Chi

The light at the end of the sunken Florida room catches my eye. The light shines through a window and sliding glass door at the back of the home, located directly across from the front door. Such a direct path means that chi passes straight through the home, taking health and fortune out of the home at the same time. A sofa is placed in this pathway, which blocks some of the exiting chi, but even more of a "dam" is needed. To gather and redirect the flow of chi, a sofa table is placed behind the sofa. Ceramic items and a plant on the table help ground the chi. The sofa table and the items on it also help create a bit of a backing for the sofa, which is important when someone must sit with his or her back to a window or door, as here. When we sit with our back exposed to a window or doorway, energy is tied up in a subconscious fight-or-flight defense. To the side of the sofa, a floor plant in a solid, earthy ceramic planter aids the blocking effort, collecting chi for redistribution throughout the home. By obscuring the rear doorway, but allowing for a two-to three-foot walkway to the right of the sofa, exiting chi is blocked and the rear door is still accessible. With these changes, a pleasant sense of vitality and balance fills the room.

Balancing the Flow to the Bedroom

The master bedroom, being to the south, falls under the Fire element, Heide's nourishing element. To augment the Fire element, touches of red can be added, which will both enhance the room's energy and nourish Heide's natal Earth element. Touches of green and blue might also be added to bring in the Wood element, the room's nourishing element.

The room's predominant colors are white and cream; it will feel more balanced with the addition of red, blue, or green. Today, Heide has red roses in her bedroom, and she enjoys having a constant supply of fresh flowers here. The clear glass vase makes the water visible, a wonderful way to bring the Water element into the bedroom. An aquarium or fountain would be far too active in this room where restful, peaceful chi energy is needed.

The master bedroom falls in the Wealth area of the ba-gua, the far left ninth of the home. The water in the clear vase and the fresh flowers are an excellent addition to the Wealth area. Metal, Water, and Wood are the elements most associated with wealth. *Shui* means "water," which is a carrier of chi. The Wood element, represented by the beautiful shapes and colors of flowers (symbols of wealth) and flourishing, lush plants symbolize growth. Just outside the angled wall of the master bedroom, we place three small, decorative evergreens in large, metal flower pots to bring more energy to the Wealth position.

Seeking Restful Sleep

Heide does not get consistently restful sleep in the master bedroom; sometimes she sleeps more soundly in the guest room. Because the head of the bed is on the same wall as the entrance to the room, we place a mirror across from the entry, angled slightly, so Heide has a view of the entrance as she lies in bed. This mirror placement helps ease the subconscious mind; knowing she can glance up to see what is going on behind her should help Heide.

Because of the arrangement of windows, the entrance to the master bath, and the sliding glass door out to the patio, the head of the bed can only go against an east wall in the master bedroom. East is not one of Heide's best four directions, so we place another small mirror to pull an image of Heide over to one of her better directions. Mirror placement is an esoteric adjustment, like a little acupuncture needle for the soul. In a bedroom, mirrors should be used sparingly because they are very activating to energy. Generally, only one mirror is recommended, and it should not hang directly across from the foot of the bed.

A Supportive Place to Work

The room where Heide works is basically a separate wing off of the main house; the work area is literally separated from the living space. Facing toward the east, this office falls under the Wood element, Heide's controlling element. To balance this, we might incorporate the control to Wood—Metal (white/silver)—or the reductive element to Wood—Fire (red).

The major problem in this office crops up again in the design of the home's second floor—wall-to-wall windows. With all these windows, chi is flying around and exiting every which way and little is staying in the home. It's a whirlwind. To remedy this, the blinds behind Heide's desk will be closed while she is working,

Heide's office

Before (left): *Heide was situated with her back to the entrance.*

After (right): *addition of a centrally placed desk places Heide in a command position and faces her in her best direction.*

and more plants will be placed in front of the windows as "protective barriers" for her back. When her back is no longer so exposed, more chi will collect around Heide and will also "cozy-up" her office in terms of energy.

Lucky Layout: The Command Position and Best Direction

Heide's desk is built into a counter and her back faces the door, not a command position. While this positioning is a bit less problematic in a home office, since you generally know who is coming and going, it still leaves much room for improvement. In a corporate office, however, sitting in a command position is imperative. If you aren't able to face the entrance with a solid wall at your back, hang a mirror that will bring the entrance into your field of vision. Heide's built-in desk looks quite commercial and doesn't match the high style she has created in other areas of her home. She is ready for a change. Checking a compass, I determine Heide is currently facing her third best direction, which isn't bad. However, her best direction is northwest. By angling a desk catercorner from the entrance, Heide will be able to face her best direction, and she will also be in a command position, having a full view of the office and the entry.

104

We choose a new Queen Anne–style desk for the office. The curving lines add some feminine, yin balance to this straight-lined room. The desk is light enough in color and style to work with the overall lightness of the room, yet it is weighty enough to ground chi, a necessity here. (A glass-topped desk would not have served the same purpose.) To further ground and augment the yin energy, a rug with some dark tones and visual depth is added. Two sets of storage cabinets in the office have about one foot of space above them. Silk greenery fills these "dead" spaces, adding visual interest.

Heide loves her new work space and immediately started placing some of her special objects on her desktop, including some of her favorite flowers, roses. The office is now much more balanced, supportive, and comfortable.

Slowing the Whirlwind

The open floor plan of the second floor is interrupted only by a central fireplace. The windows offer a 360-degree view of the ocean, mountains, and lush greenery that surround the home. As breathtaking as the views are, however, the windows don't allow the home to retain any energy. It exits constantly through the windows or up the central chimney. Recall that the center of any home or room is the Ming Tang, the most spiritually rich area—certainly not the best location for a chimney. To resolve the problem of a fireplace or wood stove located in the center of a home or room, plants might be placed around the hearth to attract and capture some of the chi energy before it exits up the flue.

Although the gorgeous vistas are striking, the home has an unsettled feeling. The walls of windows don't provide the sense of protection, peace, or balance that solid walls afford. To further complicate matters, the main seating for the second floor is built-in under the windows, forcing one's back to the windows in a less than optimum layout, with no solid structure behind the seating. The black furnishings help to absorb and hold some of the chi (black is yin and receptive), affording a bit of a respite, but for the most part the space is a whirlwind, similar to the situation in Heide's office. While on the surface it may seem desirable to have an active home, remember that the main goal of feng shui is balance. Too much activity and unbalanced energy leave us exhausted.

Addressing Many Windows

Since doors are the primary entrance for chi in a home and windows are its main exits, in the art of feng shui, there is a suggested ratio of windows to doors. Windows are the "children" and doors the "parents." The desirable ratio is no more than three windows to every door. Interior doors are included in this ratio, but only when they open into rooms, not when they open into closets or utility areas. Heide's home has a higher ratio of windows to doors, which means power is leaving the home. When windows outnumber doors, one effect is "children," or possibly employees, may not listen to the "parent," or the head of a company.

One plant placed within each grouping of three windows, as well as some hanging leaded-glass crystals, will help to moderate some of the chi. To further balance the room, blinds will be used to cut down light and glare. Formerly, the blinds remained open at all times. Now, they will be used in some areas to simulate walls for privacy, protection, and security, which should bring a pleasant sense of peace and relaxation to the space.

Orchids Represent Refinement and Endurance

The dining room and living room in this contemporary open plan are decorated and furnished in neutrals: black, white, gray, and cream. On the round dining table, Heide keeps tall, blooming orchids. Their sweeping lines, growing out of a basket of moss and dashed on one end with purple, bring an uplifting feeling and a dramatic, elegant touch of nature to the dining room. The living room falls under the Wealth position when we align the ba-gua with the entry.

In the hexagonal plan of this home, there are "missing," or cut off, corners in every room. The landscaping around the home brings life energy into all of the open, angled spaces, filling them with color, fragrance, and beauty. A sprinkler system that runs regularly sends sprays of water around the home's perimeter. Water, especially flowing water, is an excellent carrier of chi. Even the terms *current* and *currency* show a root connection. While it is preferable to have natural water on a site, often this is not possible. This "small water," or man-made water, cure is yet another method to bring moving water onto your property.

Built-in audio speakers above the bulkheads provide a sonic feng shui cure.

To the front of the home is a large grove of some fifty citrus trees, each bursting with fruit. Its placement on the ba-gua over the property covers two areas, Wisdom/General Knowledge and Career/Life Journey. The "fruit" of Heide's knowledge and career is abundant: She is a teacher, speaker, and author who has done so well in her career that she has been a guest on "Oprah!" Heide loves all the changes to her home, and says she now feels more secure and grounded, even in the midst of her career "exploding."

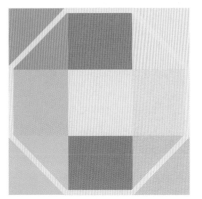

Feng Shui for the Office

Despite modernization, the aim of feng shui remains the same as it was thousands of years ago: the pursuit and creation of a more comfortable and harmonious place to live and work.
—Professor Thomas Lin Yun, *Feng Shui Master*

Marcia and Jim's business, HomeFree Funding, is an innovative company that is changing the history of home ownership for minorities. Marcia and Jim founded their company to help people find ways to buy their own homes.

Marcia noticed problems shortly after leasing the space for the new office in Washington, D.C.: "I just don't understand it. We have the same staff, but in this new location, there seems to be more stress among the eight employees. The productivity has fallen off, and another new development I'm seeing is a lack of

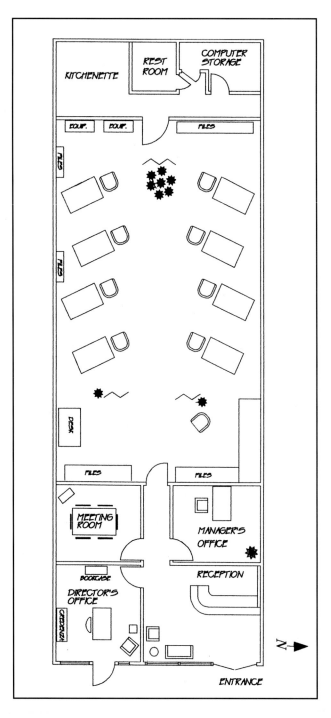

work ethic." HomeFree is doing some groundbreaking work in a fairly unusual format. (HomeFree locates funds in the private sector to help minorities afford homes.) While most companies have a very structured organization, this small company has evolved in a more organic, unfolding way. Since much of what they do has never been done before, they need to be flexible and responsive. Here, the goals of our feng shui adjustments are to reduce stress and to allow as much creative energy as possible to go into the creative growth of this innovative company.

First Impressions

On arriving at the Washington location of HomeFree, I spot some external feng shui problems that no doubt contribute to the business problems. HomeFree is the next-to-the-last business in a strip of shops and offices. At the end of the shopping center, near this office, land dips to a level a good ten to twelve feet below the level of the street. There is a depressed feeling to the area, and the front of the office is not very visible. Chi is more abundant on the higher ground. The chi that is moving and circulating rolls down the hill in a rushing, unbalanced fashion. In keeping with the specific ordinances of the location, HomeFree's exterior is not distinguished from the rest of the shopping center, making this business difficult to spot. Neither attention nor chi is attracted to the office.

Bringing the Exterior Up to Par

Better signage, with eye-catching colors, and brighter lighting should improve matters considerably. During the day, the bright colors will attract attention and chi and the lighting will handle the job at night. Color and light are two of the most powerful feng shui cures. By installing lights at ground level, aimed toward the door, chi will follow the lightwaves, being enhanced and guided into the office. This should attract many clients to HomeFree, as well as improve the health, happiness, and energy of the employees who spend eight hours a day in this office. A second set of lights aimed at the top of the roof will further raise chi, possibly elevating the chi to match the high aspirations of HomeFree.

In urban settings, theft has to be considered when choosing feng shui cures. Some of the delightful exterior feng shui adjustments—such as installation of a water fountain or placing a pair of "protective" statues on either side of the entrance—simply aren't practical here. Alternatively, we design a new sign (with colors chosen to support the east-facing entrance [Wood] and the owners' personal feng shui charts), use a few potted plants just inside and outside the front doors, and place a bright red welcome mat at the entrance to create a pleasant, inviting path for clients.

Moving Chi with Light

On this sunny afternoon, the lighting level outside seems to contrast starkly with the lower lighting level in the reception area, making the interior of the office seem darker than it actually is. Lighting represents the sun, which has a predominance of warm tones. Most fluorescent lights, which are used in this office, have a cool, almost blue-green cast—not what our eyes are used to seeing during the day. Incandescent (warm yellow) and halogen (bright white) lights are more pleasing, harmonious choices. Full-spectrum lighting is another option, but the benefits of this type of lighting are still being studied. Of course, one of the most important factors in lighting is your personal preference. If you don't like the lighting in your work space, it can be a source of constant, subtle irritation.

Marcia plans to convert the entire office to incandescent and halogen lighting, which will improve matters. For now, the reception area is much too dark. We place an incandescent lamp in the most dimly lighted corner of the room, which happens to be the Helpful People area of the ba-gua. Because all of the work performed at HomeFree involves one-on-one helpful-people relationships, the extra lighting should help support the connection between staff and potential home buyers.

Feng Shui Loves Curves

A curved reception desk sits at the edge of the Romantic Relationship/Marriage area. So many of our environments are rectilinear, straight boxes that when we introduce curves, in construction or furnishings, the result is a pleasant, harmonious feeling—something our spirits easily relate to. In *Places of the Soul*, English architect Christopher Day writes, "Curvilinear lines bring where they come from, where they go to and what they pass through into receptive conversation with each other." They balance the flow of line and energy.

In this small reception area, seating must be placed in front of a window. Blinds are kept shut to moderate chi and to provide a protective feeling for waiting clients. When vertical blinds are fully open, especially when positioned directly behind furniture, the impression is comparable to many knife edges cutting into chi. This may be moderated by leaving the blinds partially or fully closed.

The curved reception desk leads your eye around the room, past bright, colorful artwork and floral arrangements. Located in the southeast corner of the building, under the Wood element, the reception area has all five elements represented, and the feeling is inviting and comfortable. Touches of black in a vase and end table bring in Water, Wood's nourishing element. The green carpeting and the plants belong to the Wood element; the red of Fire is in the artwork; the ceramic lamp and vase bring in the Earth element; and the white walls and silver-gray furniture fall under Metal.

Calm But Moving Chi Welcomes New Clients

Across from the reception desk there is a loveseat and chair, where clients wait for their appointments. The back of the loveseat is in front of a large window and, off to the side, the front door. The vertical blinds are drawn and closed behind the loveseat, making its placement cozy and less vulnerable. Because people don't wait here long, this arrangement is fine.

Marcia's office, located in the front left corner, falls under the Wisdom/General Knowledge area of the ba-gua, an appropriate location for a director. Her desk faces one of her top four directions, and she sits in a command position, backed by a solid wall. Marcia has full view of, but is not in line with, the entrance to her office.

In Marcia's office and the reception area, there is an unusual construction feature. Immediately in front of the windows, the ceiling is nine feet high. Moving into the room one foot, the ceiling height drops to eight feet, creating an alcove of sorts at the ceiling level. Chi could collect and stagnate in this area. To remedy this, part of the alcove might be mirrored or a mobile or plant hung to draw the chi down to a more human level. If a mirror is used, it won't actually be seen in this alcove. It is not necessary for a mirror to be seen for it to enhance the movement of chi. If we consider a ba-gua placed just over Marcia's office, we discover that by hanging a plant in the Family/Health position, this area will receive two feng shui adjustments in one: The living plant will enhance and move chi, and green will support the Family/Health area.

In the small conference room, an easel is placed at an angle in the far left corner. A table with a pink and rose floral arrangement is in the Romantic Relationship/Marriage area, the far right corner, and is angled in the opposite direction. These simple touches give the room a vital feeling. Angles of any type in fabrics, murals, and especially furniture placed at an angle in a corner, increase the dynamic sense of movement in a space. The rectangular (Earth element) conference table in the center of the room grounds the energy to support the daily meetings that take place there.

The Director's Office
Marcia sits in a command position that affords full view of her office. Flowers decorate the Wealth area.

Octagons—Balanced Shapes

Octagons are the luckiest, most auspicious shape in feng shui: They are a combination of the circle and square. The circle represents heaven, the square symbolizes earth, and the octagon is a combination of the two. An octagonal clock hangs in the conference room, and octagonal plant stands are used in the reception area and in the managing director's office.

Jerome, the managing director, was born under the Earth element, making Fire his nourishing element. Jerome wants red walls in his office, but because he meets with clients, some nervous about their first step toward purchasing a home, he must consider how they might react to a room with red walls. Instead, a shade of red, such as pink, rose, or mauve, can be used on one or two walls and for the upholstered chairs. These tones reduce the intensity of the Fire element when it is used in large areas. Jerome can then use his vibrant red in smaller doses—in planters, accent furniture, and artwork.

Jerome's office falls under the Helpful People/Travel area of the ba-gua. The colors used to enhance the Helpful People/Travel area are black (for wisdom and depth), white, and gray (for communication). In Jerome's office, the walls are white, an octagonal pedestal is black, and gray in the artwork and planter complete the supportive scheme. This certainly helps Jerome's position as the managing director, both in his interactions with the staff and with the clients of HomeFree.

Pooling Chi

The main office is huge, measuring some thirty feet wide by fifty feet long. Arranged as an open floor plan, you can walk right into the space of eight busy employees. One of the biggest problems in the office is this: Good fortune, along with chi, can rush straight through the main office—not circulating along the sides of the room where people work—because a rear door is directly across from the entrance. Marcia thought that was a good feature in such a large open space. She even hung a painting on the wall in the opening beyond the rear doorway, to frame the piece, thinking it attracted people's attention. All that did was to take even more focus out of the main office. To remedy this, chi must be pooled or gathered to benefit the employees.

Nature always comes to mind when I look for an especially potent cure. Interior landscaping with houseplants became popular in the early 1970s and has

Before (top):
This large, uninterrupted open office plan lacked privacy.

After (bottom):
The introduction of screens and potted plants at the front and rear doorways accommodated better circulation of chi.

remained an important part of decorating. Humans used to spend much more time outdoors, and we seem to have lost touch, literally, with an important part of life. Mother earth has a healing force all her own, and some of her natural bounty, such as plants, flowers, and water, when brought inside, remind us of our elemental connection to nature.

Office work is classified under the Earth element because it is often routine. All offices benefit from the inclusion of both the Earth element and its nourishing element, Fire. Adding plants (Wood element) to an office helps instill a creative feeling in what might seem a predictable routine.

To pool the chi, we place five large plants in front of an oriental folding screen, about four feet in front of the rear exit. The predominant color on the folding screen is gold, the Earth element. There is sufficient space to move around the plant/screen arrangement, but you can no longer stand at the front of the office and see straight out of the exit. The energy shifts dramatically. Immediately, the feeling of the office seems warmer, more welcoming.

To distribute the chi, we angle all the desks for two reasons: (1) to enliven the "mood" of the room with dynamic diagonals, and (2) to mimic the top half of the octagon with the desks. In this configuration, everyone sits in a command position, facing the entrance, not just the back of the person in front of them.

To enhance and spread the business reputation of HomeFree, we place a beautiful, gold, open-metalwork floor lamp in the Fame/Advancement area. Artwork will be chosen to include the colors related to each area of the ba-gua in which it will be hung. This process is a subtle, conscious mandala to augment every area of life for the staff on a daily basis and to surround the clients with beautiful artwork of many colors.

As a final adjustment to the main office, we situate two partitions near the front of the open, large office to create a small area that includes a comfortable chair. This passageway shields the direct view to the employees, providing a little more privacy and, at the same time, creating a small, interesting space that will be used as a lobby for clients. All of these changes combined reduce the large, open space to a more human scale.

Arguing Doors

The back center ninth in an office or home is the Fame/Advancement area. At HomeFree, an odd circumstance called "arguing doors" occurs in the back center of the building. Two doors open toward one another and the doorknobs hit. This occurs in about 10 percent of homes and offices. The arguing doors suggest an increased probability of arguments occurring, either at home, in friendships, or at work. The lack of harmony Marcia has seen recently in her staff should shift after we rectify these knocking doorknobs. The cure consists of cutting a piece of red ribbon in an increment of nine inches. Generally, twenty-seven or thirty-six inches are necessary to reach between the two doors. Tie an end of the ribbon to each of the two doorknobs. Do the three transcendental cures, (see chapter 6), making the creative visualization step specific to the employees, or in the case of a home, to the inhabitants. Then cut the ribbon in the middle, tie it into bows around the doorknobs, and leave it in place. The red color of the ribbon symbolically (and energetically) holds back the tension of this undesirable design.

The Process of Feng Shui

Marcia and her staff are happy with their adjusted work spaces and are intrigued by the depth of feng shui. Although many of the changes were simple, everyone feels and comments on the improvements. Feng shui unfolds as an ongoing process. HomeFree is already planning for the expansion of this office and has offices slated for other cities, with feng shui support in each one.

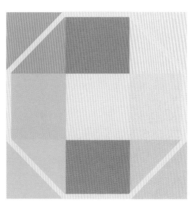

Penthouse Apartment
New York, New York

Many look for their Shangri-la on the surface of the earth, others voyage within for illumination. The ancient Chinese art of feng shui combines the axes of each quest, declaring that what you make of your location and environment on the face of the earth also affects your inner peace.

—Stephen Skinner, *Writer*

Jane and Jonathan, owners of a duplex penthouse apartment on Park Avenue on the Upper East Side of New York City, want feng shui to guide their renovations. They wish to create a home that represents their spirit and love.

After Jane and Jonathan purchased their home and moved in, Jane's mother became terminally ill. At the time, Jane was working with decorators, but, under-

Feng Shui, Past and Present

For centuries after its inception, feng shui was primarily used to locate ideal gravesites for deceased relatives. In the East, much emphasis is placed on ancestral worship, not only out of respect, but also to facilitate the inheritance of chi and blessings from one's ancestors. Today, feng shui is practiced more often for the living, to uplift and balance the flow of chi in and around homes to create harmonious surroundings.

standably, she couldn't focus on the project. She left for England to be with her mother, communicating many of her final design decisions by phone.

Jane's mother died, family matters were settled, and Jane, filled with grief, returned home. To say she was unpleasantly surprised by the look of her newly decorated home would be an understatement. The library was too dark, the decoration of her office was too formal and impractical, and the accessories in the house were flashy and ornate—not at all suitable to her tastes. After much expense and three years' time, Jane now needs to create the home environment she envisions for herself, her husband, their three children, and the child they are expecting.

One Major Change at a Time

Renovations should be kept simple during a time of pregnancy. Extensive building projects and carrying a child both take enormous amounts of energy. Feng shui suggests taking on only one creative, life-changing event at a time, otherwise chi might potentially be taken from the baby. For this reason, major renovations will be done after the child is born.

Personal Elements

To begin, we must establish the personal elements for each family member. Jane, Jonathan, and their son Alexander were all born under the yang Metal element. In the Five Element Configuration (see chapter 11), Jonathan is lacking the Earth and Water elements. Because Earth is his nourishing element, it is especially important for the Earth element to be included in his physical environment. Jane is lacking the Water element. Adding the Water element to the home will help Jane and Jonathan both feel more deeply at ease, especially in the emotional realm. Alex is not lacking any element in his Five Element Configuration, so no additional compensation is necessary for balance. He does not have the Earth element on a specific line in his Five Element Configuration, but he has the other four; that combination grants him the Earth element, as explained in chapter 11.

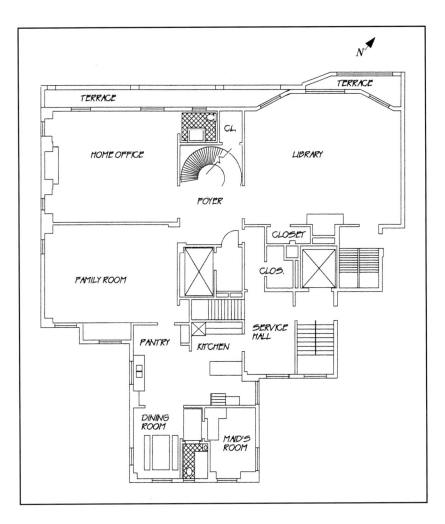

Juliette, the eldest daughter, was born under the Wood element and is missing Wood and Earth in her Five Element Configuration. We will work to bring her missing elements into her bedroom. The youngest daughter, Delilah, was born under the Earth element, which is nourished by Fire; both these elements are missing from her personality configuration chart. We will enhance these missing elements in her surroundings, particularly since they are her natal and nourishing elements.

Part of the Home's First Impression

Jane's office is located in a room immediately off the foyer. At first, she says, it seemed like a great idea. But the fact is, the messiest room in the house is the one you see when you first come in, and with children coming and going, the door is seldom shut. The office has an unusual double-sided desk that allows access from either side; it's part of a built-in bookcase on the center wall. Typically, double desks are twice as deep as single desks, but Jane's desk is only marginally wider than a single desk. She admits that she's never liked the custom desk. The rattan inserts in the drawer fronts are frayed, indicating that it's time to repair or replace this item. When a visitor uses the phone at the desk, there is no privacy. Also, the children work on the computer here.

Private Spaces

Jane spends a lot of time in the office "administrating" the family, their finances, and the logistics of life and recently moved a lot of their home business information into her husband's office. She wants to separate business from home as much as possible and hopes to write biographies. Presently, there is no space set up to support her writing.

Carving out a niche for Jane to claim as her own will be relatively easy in this spacious room, which is twenty three feet long by fourteen feet wide, but first the built-in desk must go. The design of the desk is not particularly attractive, and Jane simply doesn't like it. Remember, if you don't love it, replace it!

Using a folding screen to divide the room in half, we create a secluded space for Jane toward the back of the room. We refer to her best four directions to determine how a new desk should be situated, once positioned behind the folding screen. There is a beautiful fireplace on the back wall of the office, and Jane imagines how much she will enjoy building a fire and sitting down to work at her nearby desk. Jane also quickly realizes how perfect this new area will be for a glass-front cabinet she inherited from her parents. It will give her a place to put small mementos and a collection of enamel eggs, special belongings that are currently scattered about her home. The assorted colors of the enamel eggs will enhance the Wealth area beautifully.

Two armchairs and a loveseat moved closer to the entrance of the office create a separate conversation area. Complete with a telephone on a small coffee table, this spot is a welcoming reception area, available for visitors' use yet separate from Jane's work.

Adjacent to the office is a room originally designed as a wet bar that now serves as a plant-potting area; it is filled with orchids resting between blooms. Between the office and the den, we place a comfortable chair for Jane. When she has the time, Jane enjoys sitting in this chair to knit, in close proximity to her children's play area.

Making Rooms Fit Your Lifestyle

The children's computer will be relocated to the den, a room that gets a lot of use as a family room and playroom. This change places the computer in the General Knowledge/Wisdom area, an excellent place to study. In the apartment's original design, the den was a formal dining room; it's located next to the kitchen. The first night the dining room was used as a family room, Alex felt sick, and he laid on the sofa near to Jane as she prepared dinner in the kitchen. This confirmed for Jane that the new use for the room was appropriate.

Contemporary living needs differ from those of previous generations; they also vary from person to person and from family to family. To determine if your rooms are being used well, list all the activities you would like to carry out at home. Then, begin to search for ways to support the life you want to live. Careful evaluation of Jane's young family revealed a greater need for an exercise room, a music room, and a playroom for the children than a formal dining room.

Room for the Mind to Rest

Jane's biggest concern is to simplify: She feels there are too many things, too many ornaments, too much furniture, too much technology. As she puts it, "In my dream life, we'd be living somewhere that's very Japanese—not many possessions, very white, clean, and plain. But in reality, it's important to me to keep around the things that people have given us and the things that belonged to my parents and to other people we care about. I'm always feeling in conflict about these two options."

This is a common dilemma. Spouses, partners, and roommates often differ in the level of clutter and possessions they prefer. My standard rule of thumb is less than 50 percent of a space should be filled. This includes floor space, wall space, counter space, and the area on top of a desk. Visually, the mind needs space to go and rest: It loves the contrast between active and passive, decorated and plain, occupied and open. Fifty percent openness may be balanced between different planes as well. For example, a room with less furniture can work nicely with more than fifty percent of its wall space filled with art. Balance allows for collections of special belongings and peace of mind.

In China and Japan, visual clutter is reduced to a figure much lower than fifty percent. Books and utilitarian items such as electronics are often concealed in cabinets, behind screens, or behind beautiful fabrics. These may be options for Jane in the family room. A big-screen television, a large collection of CDs, and a deluge of toys fill the room. A storage unit for the television and music, and two storage units for toys will effectively reduce the visual clutter. Floor-to-ceiling shelves surrounding the television, hidden behind sliding decorative shoji screens, are another possible option, but cabinet storage will better suit the style of the home's furnishings.

L-Shaped Rooms

Many apartments and homes have two rooms that are open to each other in an L-shaped layout. The kitchen and dining area of Jane's home is arranged in this fashion. Jane first noticed the L when Juliette was a baby. When she sat in her high chair at the table and couldn't see her mother in the kitchen, she'd start screaming and howling. With a toddler still using a high chair and a new baby on the way, a solution is needed.

In this kitchen, the stove (Fire element) and sink (Water element) are in line with each other. The decorative metal sheet hung on the cabinet edge near the sink provides a barrier between these two elements.

Black Hat feng shui offers a way to unite the energies of any two rooms in an L-shaped configuration—a plant placed at the corner that connects the dining room and kitchen. This central spot is the intersection of the angles of the two rooms. In addition to the plant, strategically hanging a mirror to pull an image of Jane into the dining area will provide a way for the children to see their mom when she is in the kitchen. Another option that will meet the needs of Jane's young ones would be to add a small counter at the end of the island in the kitchen. There is just enough room to fit one stool and a high chair for the children so they can watch their mother or babysitter prepare food.

The dining area is to the north, the Water element, and falls under the Career/Life Journey area of the ba-gua. The room is small, so adding a mirror will open up and expand the area visually, as well as providing a feng shui cure. Hanging a mirror in the dining room, especially when it reflects (and visually doubles) the number of dishes you have, symbolically doubles your wealth. The same holds true when hanging a mirror behind your stove; the doubled burners from the reflection symbolically means doubled food and doubled wealth.

In this home, the kitchen falls under the Career/Life Journey area of the ba-gua. A mirror placed here can increase the opportunities in both Jane's and Jonathan's careers. When hanging a mirror, care must be taken not to "cut into" the heads of any family members, short or tall. It is sometimes better to hang a small, decorative mirror than a large one, particularly so diners won't have to watch themselves throughout a meal.

A New Library

The final room on the main floor was originally the living room. It is now a library and music room, and Jonathan's favorite. He is in the publishing business, and he and Jane have quite a collection of valuable books. Interestingly, when I first walked into the library, I noticed a beautiful black lacquered upright piano to the left of the entrance. The black color very nicely supports the Career/Life Journey area where it sits. Across the room, in the Fame position, is an antique rolltop desk. On a deep level, the desk seems heavy and out of place to me. I suggest we reverse the two pieces, placing the piano in the Fame position and the desk in the Career/Life Journey position. The bookshelves now look like they were custom-built with an alcove for the piano. To the right of the piano, in the Romantic Relationship/Marriage corner, Jonathan has his guitars, stereo, and collector's LPs. The music is grouped together in an inviting arrangement for the musicians in the family.

The library has so many items—too many, it seems. Jane must rid the room of those things she does not love to create more room for flowing chi and items her family will appreciate. A lightness develops as we begin removing the objects that are not loved by Jane and her family—items such as highly embellished lamps, antique metal sculptures of spiked plants, and other ornate accessories.

Furniture Around the Ba-gua

When planning the seating arrangement in a room, I start with two criteria: (1) I want to take advantage of a command position, catercorner to the entrance of the room, and (2) I want the seating to face the best directions for the inhabitants.

In the library, the command position fulfills both requirements. For this reason, we place the sofa catercorner to the entrance. After the sofa is in place, I realize the intriguing possibility of arranging the rest of the furniture to follow the shape of the ba-gua. We angle chairs on either side of the fireplace and place chairs and tables across from them. This configuration encourages your eye to travel around the room; it is the embodiment of movement, flow, and openness. At once, the library seems lighter and brighter.

Keeping Chi in Motion

Behind the bookshelves are some extra shelves, stored on the floor in front of a closed-off door that leads to an elevator, no longer in use. When items simply sit without being used, they deaden the chi of a room. We move the stored shelves out of the library, a main living space, and into a remote storage closet. Because the elevator door still exists but is not used, a mirror placed on the back of a bookshelf, in front of the door, will allow chi to move around the closed-off area.

There are three elevators in this suite: (1) a service elevator that leads up to the penthouse, (2) the library elevator that is no longer used, and (3) the main entrance elevator. The main elevator comes up through the center of the home. Such placement is not problematic for a business, as it assists in the dissemination of energy to different floors; however, in a home where one of the main desires is to nourish the soul, the center or Ming Tang is ideally open, an unobstructed vehicle for the free movement of energy.

Ming Tang—The Heart of the Home

In the Ming Tang, or center of a home, an elevator, bathroom, kitchen, and fireplace are not desirable. To adjust any of the situations, mirrors or plants should be carefully placed to increase the amount of chi available for the family.

To remedy the central location of the elevator in this home, we hang mirrors on the walls in the vestibule between the elevator and front door, install new lighting to increase chi, and add a plant to bring in a touch of nature. Two small lion-figure doorstops stand on either side of the front door as guardians, a perfect in-scale touch for the small vestibule.

Light and Moving Water for the Foyer

The dried hydrangeas in a beautiful red vase create a new focal point while they conceal the firebox.

Jonathan has never liked the foyer, and he specifically doesn't like the lack of light. We move a collage of photographs to a new location in the foyer to make room for a mirror that will be placed directly across from the entrance. In front of the mirror, a halogen floor lamp brightens the once dark space under the stairwell. A stone, trickling water fountain, added to the foyer to supplement Jane and Jonathan's missing Water element, creates a lively, welcoming first impression.

A beautiful antique carved wooden cherub hangs just below a tall window, in the winding staircase. She seems to be a guardian angel for the home. Upstairs, in the large penthouse, are the bedrooms.

Cultivating Chi in the Bedroom

The many windows and doorways in the master bedroom leave only two walls against which the bed may be placed. The bed will be in a command position, but neither the door into the bedroom nor the head of the bed faces one of Jane or Jonathan's top four directions. Jane wonders if this situation should prompt a move. It seems perhaps that a few years down the road they might wish to consider moving. If people are *truly* happy with their homes, they do not question whether they want to move. If in doubt, ask yourself, Do I love this home? If you cannot answer yes with all your heart, perhaps you should move. For now, work with feng shui adjustments to make a balanced and supportive living environment for yourself, one that will help everyone feel happy and will usher in, at the suitable time, the support and circumstances necessary for any appropriate changes.

We begin the master bedroom adjustments by hanging a crystal between the master bath and the master bedroom. From the bed, the toilet is in sight, signaling very poor feng shui. When we sleep, we are at our most vulnerable. Our human chi mixes with chi in the room and is at risk of going "down the drain." When the toilet is visible directly from the bed, the negative effects are heightened. Closing the door to the bathroom is one possible correction. Another pos-

Before effecting a feng shui cure, this foyer was very dark. Now, the brighter entry area is loved by everyone in the family.

sibility might be a half-wall alongside the toilet to shield it from view. Jane thinks the privacy wall is a wonderful idea. This may be created either with construction in drywall or glass block, or with a fabric panel. One such solution was created beautifully with a width of damask fabric that matched the bath decor.

A folding screen is mounted on the wall behind the bed. In feng shui, it is desirable not to have anything too heavy over the bed. The physical weight and "energetic" mass of heavy items symbolize undue pressure over your head while you sleep. It is better to have a small to medium-sized work of art, or nothing, directly over the bed. However, larger artwork to the sides of the bed is fine. Jane decides she'll find a new place for the screen downstairs.

Directly across from the bed are three windows. Large metal urns holding plants are placed in front of the first and third windows, and do an excellent job mediating the rushing river of chi. The plants, along with a chaise angled in front of the windows, will help create a calmer feeling in the room. A mirror sitting off to the side pulls an image of Jane and John to one of their top four directions. A reminder: Never place a mirror directly opposite the foot of the bed.

The fireplace in the master bedroom will be enhanced with either a floral arrangement in the opening or a painted screen. Typically, a mirror over a mantle is desirable, but not in this bedroom. One mirror is already in place and, ideally, only one mirror will be used in a bedroom. The goal is to create a calm, restful haven, and mirrors enhance moving, active chi.

Symbolism in Artwork

When I first saw the master bedroom, there was a painting hanging over the fireplace of a woman lying alone on a bed. The painting was done in neutral tones, in the style of a Matisse cutout. Jane found the painting peaceful, and it is quite beautiful and captivating. The symbology, however, doesn't seem appropriate for a couple's bedroom. All of the shapes of color are segregated—nothing overlaps—and the figure lies alone on a bed. Jane hangs the painting in another room and replaces it with a lovely, original Andrew Wyeth watercolor of a grouping of trees in a winter scene. She and Jonathan, both born under the Metal element, will benefit from the predominance of white in the Wyeth.

Jane has never felt completely pleased with the master bedroom in this apartment. After her baby is born, she plans a major renovation of the bedroom suite and changes to the entry location and bed placement to further align the room using feng shui recommendations.

Children's Rooms

With a new baby on the way, the children's bedrooms will be changing. Delilah and Juliette will share a room with a lot of Wood energy from the color blue and the mural of trees. The Wood energy will nicely support these growing girls, especially Juliette who was born under the Wood element. However, to support Delilah's natal Earth element, the Metal element (which controls Wood) or the Fire element (which reduces Wood) must be included to create balance and some breathing room for her Earth energy.

The bedroom Juliette is moving out of will become the nursery. When the baby is born, new colors for the room will be chosen from the child's natal and nourishing elements. To soften a projecting corner, we place a green plant on a shelf to grow up along the corner's edge.

We change the arrangement of Alex's bedroom, moving his head placement from one of his worst directions to his second best direction. A new computer desk faces in Alex's best direction. Bookcases have also been added, changing the look of the room from a little boy's to one with support for his expanding interests and his hockey memorabilia.

Jane, Jonathan, and the children cannot believe how pleasant their home feels. The library seems like an entirely different room, and there is a coziness in this large, two-story apartment that was missing before. Jane is spending time doing some of her favorite hobbies and relaxing more. She also finds she has more time to spend with her children, making everyone quite happy.

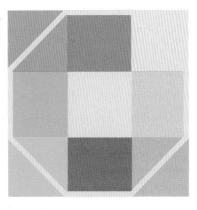

Brookfield Farm
Ontario, Canada

Without leaving my house I know the whole universe.
—Lao-Tzu, *Philosopher*

This Ontario home, called Brookfield Farm, sits on one hundred acres of land. At one point, it was a colt farm owned by E. P. Taylor, a breeder of champion race horses. Originally constructed in a rectangular shape, an addition built in the 1950s gave the home its present L shape. Feng shui adjustments can balance the irregular shape with landscaping, and with wind chimes placed in the missing Helpful People/Travel area of the ba-gua.

Since previously I had never traveled to Canada, I expected a few feet of snow to be on the ground during this midwinter trip. I arrived in-between snowstorms, however, and the six inches of snow on the ground allowed me to walk around the property to get a sense of the land and the flow of the chi, and to feel the peacefulness of this rural site where Linda and her partner Barry live.

Linda is an incredible illustrator. (She created the rich images for the Five Elements included in chapter 2.) Barry is a cinematographer; they both have studios in Toronto.

Choosing a Home Site

Barry and Linda are at an exciting place in their lives. They are searching for their first piece of property and plan to build their ideal home from the ground up, complete with feng shui. We examined five parcels of land, but none met feng shui criteria. Many were on sharply sloped hills (where the chi rolls off too quickly), two were at the end of dead-end streets (where chi is often stagnant), and one sold just days before. A few of these parcels were being repossessed by banks—clues that the previous owners faced financial difficulties—and are probably not appropriate for this reason.

Because he and Linda were going to move in a year or two, Barry wasn't sure whether it would be worthwhile to put any money or energy into their current home. I explained that a balanced environment might bring forward the next phase of their life together more quickly and perhaps more gracefully. Feng shui can increase luck in a person's life, even though it may not change one's destiny. With luck, anything is possible, including finding the perfect property.

Making It Easier for Chi to Enter

Oddly enough, on the home's new addition, the screen door and the front door are hinged on opposite sides. Barry has solved the problem temporarily by dismantling the screen door's closing mechanism. Still, there is an awkwardness when you open the screen door on the right and have to reach across to open the front door's handle on the left. Rehanging the screen door hinges on the right will streamline movements, making it easier for people and chi to enter. Just as Barry and Linda will struggle less to enter through the doors, so will chi. Accessible openings allow an abundance of graceful energy to flow into the home.

The screen and front doors are hinged on opposite sides, which creates a cumbersome entrance to the home.

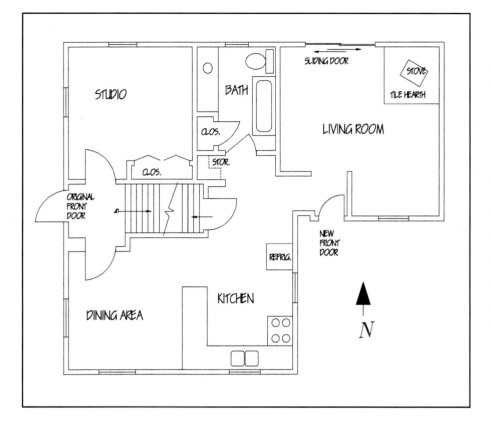

Once inside, Barry mentions how inconvenient it is to have a small mudroom, and, being a cinematographer, how difficult it is to carry his camera bags past hanging coats and a piece of furniture used for storage. Because Barry and Linda are designing their next home, I suggest including a large mudroom, complete with all the storage necessary for the items they use in their work. With thoughts of ample storage dancing through his head, Barry seems ready to build tomorrow. For the time being, though, moving some of the out-of-season coats elsewhere and replacing the storage furniture with a smaller piece will clear a path for people and chi to pass through more easily.

Entering the front door and standing in the mudroom, I see a wall directly across from me that stops partway in the front-door opening. My left eye focuses on the wall, and my right eye looks through the living room to patio doors located at the rear of the house. To remedy this, we hang a mirror on the left wall close to the edge of the opening, creating more symmetry and providing more light and openness in this small entranceway. Another option might be to cut the existing wall in half, which will give the illusion of more area in the entry, while at the same time providing wall space against which a short bookcase might be placed in the living room.

Following the Chi

On leaving the mudroom, my attention is pulled equally to the left and to the right. This is good, as it means chi is active in both areas. However, because the living room has sliding glass doors at the back of the house that are in direct alignment with the front door, chi rushes through the house too quickly. A small rosemary plant sits in front of the glass doors next to a wrought iron bin filled with firewood. Cut wood doesn't have the same life force as the Wood energy of living plants, and so it does little to capture chi. Linda replaces the small plant with a larger rosemary plant on a stand, which will help ground the rushing chi.

A pane of glass in the patio door is cracked, perhaps a visual sign of the chi energy rushing through. Because Barry and Linda lease this home, the cost of replacing the glass door must be considered carefully. When a physical repair is not feasible, a symbolic feng shui cure may be used. A *symbolic cure* is an unusual feng shui adjustment and relies totally on intention. The symbolic, intention-based adjustment suggested for this broken glass is a red decal, a dot of red paint, or a red-dot seal (the kind you might find at an office stationery store) placed directly over the crack to hold the broken energy in its place. Of all colors, red has the slowest wavelength, and is one of the most physically energizing. The color red helps to ground energy and, at the same time, can resist negativity. The symbolic repair is enhanced with the three transcendental cures (see chapter 6).

Deflecting Sha

Just outside the sliding glass door, a handrail rests on top of a lattice fence surrounding a deck and hot tub. The handrail follows a straight line at the edge of the deck for about twelve feet and ends pointing at the center of the glass door. This is an example of sha, or negative chi, sometimes called a *secret arrow*. Anything sharp or angled that points toward your door or window carries a stream of negative energy along its path, like an unseen arrow. To diffuse sha, a new focal point must be created: in this case, perhaps a small plant placed to trail over the end of the handrail.

Linda mentions that the sliding glass door has really become a problem this winter. They use the door only to bring in firewood and for access to the hot tub, but often the door's plastic rollers get jammed. It's too cold to remove the door for repair. The broken, jammed door falls in the Fame area of the ba-gua, suggesting perhaps that the door to fame, or the advancement of the inhabitants' business opportunities, may not be moving easily, requiring extra effort on their part.

Opening to Increased Fame

Barry and Linda are accomplished artists in their early forties. They are self-employed and have paid their dues for a number of years, firmly establishing their careers. Linda's drawings and paintings are represented in Canada, the United States, France, Japan, and the Far East. Barry travels around the world filming for a number of clients, including the Discovery Channel. While they have done well and are quite successful, they both feel there is room for some growth. It seems to me that Barry and Linda's careers are expanding and that their fame is on the rise, trying to break new ground. By repairing the door and attending to the crack in the glass, Barry and Linda will invite more fame into their lives, even with a symbolic cure.

Love in the Home

The Romantic Relationship/Marriage area of the ba-gua falls in the far right corner of the living room, which is also the far right corner of the house, making this a "double" Romantic Relationship/Marriage corner. Here, there is a beautiful wood stove that gets used often in the cold Canadian climate. It is angled in the corner of the room and has a full-view glass door. The dancing fire catches my eye, and the angled placement is dynamic, as it gracefully moves chi and invites further exploration of that part of the room. A bonsai tree that has seen better days should be placed in an out-of-the-way nook in the home, where it can be nursed back to health, not in the main living area. Linda removes the devitalized plant to a spot near a window in the basement, and a healthy plant remains in the Romantic Relationship/Marriage area.

Linda's artwork enhances the walls of the living room. Because of the heat, it is difficult to hang artwork behind a wood stove, but without it it looks a bit bare. Decorative pottery or plates—ideally in the Romantic Relationship/Marriage colors of red, pink, and white—might be hung in this area to support Barry and Linda's relationship. A pair of brown ceramic pots, currently holding willow branches, resides to the right of the wood stove. Pairs of items are desirable in the Romantic Relationship/Marriage area, as they represent the couple. For any flowers, the water must be kept clean and fresh. Water has many symbolic levels, including the depths of ourselves and our emotions.

"Interest" in the Wealth Corner

Barry's favorite armchair sits in the living room, the Wealth area of the ba-gua located to the north of the home's center, which places it under the Water element, Barry's natal element. He enjoys sitting here to read, relax, converse, or to listen to music. Water is nourished by Metal, and this area is enhanced by both

color (the white walls and sheer white drapery) and materials (a metal lamp and wrought-iron fire-wood bin). Barry's favorite chair faces one of his best directions. A reading light and the large rosemary plant enhance the area. The most interesting feng shui symbol in this corner is a pastel drawing done by Linda of a landscape with rolling hills, assorted Canadian trees, and a large lake. The colors of the piece are primarily blue, purple, and green, all Wealth col-

Barry's easy chair and ottoman, which face one of his best directions, supply a comfortable resting spot in his natal Water element area (north).

ors. The water in the drawing symbolizes the Water element, which connotes money, and the trees symbolize growth. The Wealth position in the living room is very nicely supported.

Decorating for a Purpose

On the other side of the living room, a sofa placed at a slight angle in an alcove covers the Helpful People and Career/Life Journey areas. This is where Linda prefers to sit. Here she faces one of her best directions, north. The only problem, according to feng shui, is the window's location behind the sofa; a window does

Artwork and a lamp augment the Children/Creative Projects area of the living room. Greenery behind the sofa creates a level of subconscious security when someone sits with their back toward the window.

not create a protective backing, something always favored for primary seating. We place a plant table behind the sofa and arrange an assortment of green plants, filling in the open area behind the sofa and the bottom half of the window. This adjustment creates the needed feeling of security for the subconscious mind. By averting a primal "fight or flight" response, more energy is made available for creativity.

In many areas, we often have items already in place that can serve as feng shui cures. A lamp with a white shade, and a beautiful pastel done by Linda that uses a lot of white and has a white mat, reside in the middle of the right wall in the living room. This is the Children/Creative Projects area of the ba-gua, which is represented by the color white. The artwork and the lamp already in place may be used to augment this position once Linda and Barry establish their hopes for the creative projects in their lives. For these items truly to work as feng shui cures, Linda and Barry "potentize" them with the three transcendental cures (see chapter 6).

Ensouling Our Environments

Barry and Linda have many beautiful, decorative items throughout their home. Immediately upon my arrival I felt a wholeness and a continuity. Linda shared that she is always on the lookout for pieces that speak to her, belongings that seem special. It took Linda and Barry four years to craft their surroundings. The soul of a home develops slowly over time and shows itself in many facets.

Slowing Down the Exit of Chi

To the left of the living room is a storage area that Linda knows to be a problem. It has floor-to-ceiling shelves that are open yet very dark. This storage area is just outside the bathroom. Standing in this area elicits a strange feeling, both congested and unsettled at the same time. Stepping back, I see all the variables responsible for this unease. Starting at the front of the home and in a direct line through to the back of the home, we see the following: a window, the entrance to the storage area, the entrance to the bathroom, and a window on the back wall in the bathroom. Together, these four openings create a too fast–moving lane of chi, somewhat like a railroad train. To remedy this, we place a mirror on the side wall of the storage area. This pulls some chi over to the side and brings light to the area, preventing the chi from stagnating in the mini-alcove. Above the storage area, we hang a mobile made of round, leaded-glass crystals. The crystals literally get things moving, reflecting and dispersing chi more evenly.

A lovely arrangement of three potted ranunculus plants with huge white flowers sits in the bathroom window. The (odd) number three is yang and connotes action. Having these plants in the window helps capture some of the chi from the "fast lane" of openings. This situation calls for all the moderations we can muster.

"Missing Corner" Cures

In the front left corner of the bathroom is a closet, just to the left of the doorway. This is the Wisdom/General Knowledge area of the bathroom. The closet cre-

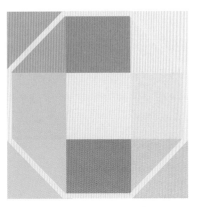

Establishing Your Personal Feng Shui Palette

Astrology is a science in itself and contains an illuminating body of knowledge. It taught me many things, and I am greatly indebted to it. Geophysical evidence reveals the power of the stars and the planets in relation to the terrestrial. In turn, astrology is like a life-giving elixir to mankind.

—Albert Einstein, *Nobel Prize–Winning Physicist, Humanist*

This chapter sets forth many rules. However, do not be bound by these rules. Instead, use this information to involve your insight, intuition, and inspiration when designing your living environments. Establish the elemental information for yourself, family members, and friends. Then, using the information on the compass directions explained here and in chapter 2, study the elements governing the orientations of each of your rooms. Look for ways to bring an individual's nourishing elements into prominence or to bring balance to a room. (See chart 2, on pages 150–53 for suggestions.)

The Pa-Kua Compass Directions and the Natal Element

We begin with Chinese astrology and the Five Element Configuration. These systems will provide insight and information necessary for you to understand how the five elements and yin/yang energy are present in your personal profile. The Asian healing arts seldom work in a homeopathic way, with like treating like. Rather, Asian systems generally work by creating a state of balance. For example, if one's chart is predominantly yang, an effort is made to bring in more yin energy and vice versa. Balance is also created within the five elements. If one or more of the five elements is absent from your personal profile, seek ways to enhance your home and support your life with a complete representation and a balance of the five elements.

Directions precede each step and each chart. Be patient with this information: It is both simple and deep, and the depth of this knowledge becomes part of your understanding only gradually.

Creating Your Chart

This blank chart can be photocopied for your use, or you may simply list your personal element information on a sheet of paper, using the same sequence. Consider this your personal palette. You will find a completed sample chart for Luciano Pavarotti at the end of this chapter.

The Five Element Configuration
To complete this section, use the information found in charts 3, 6, 7, 8, and 9.
Year of birth:_____ Natural element of your animal sign:_____
Element of your birth hour:_____ Element of your birth month:_____
Element of your birth country:_____

Pa-Kua Compass Directions

Chart 3 lists the pa-kua annual numbers for each year; years differ for males and females. You will find the associated compass directions for your pa-kua number in chart 4.

Pa-kua number:_____

Compass directions listed from best to worst:_____

Feng Shui Natal Element

Your natal element is your deepest core energy. Your nourishing element nourishes your natal element. Both are highly supportive when used in your living environments. Charts 3 and 5 provide information to help you compute your natal element. Cross-reference your pa-kua number from chart 3 with your month of birth on chart 5 to establish your natal element.

Refer to the nourishing cycle diagram in chapter 1 (page 14) to learn your nourishing element, the element that precedes your natal element in the cycle.

Natal element:_____   Nourishing element:_____

The first system, the Five Element Configuration, consists of five lines of information related to the date, time, and location of your birth; each will be associated with one of the five elements.

After noting the data associated with your birth, check to see whether both yin and yang are represented. If your birth information is all yin or all yang, see chart 1, The World of Yin/Yang: Achieving Balance, for suggestions on how to establish the balance.

Filling in Your Personal Palette

First, find your birth year in chart 3, Yearly Elements, and record a yin or yang year, as appropriate. Then, note the element governing your year of birth. Your birth year was ruled by one of the twelve animal signs, each of which has its own natural element (see chart 6, Natal Elements of the Twelve Animal Signs). Record your ruling animal and its natural element.

Your hour of birth is referenced to the animal sign and element that rules each two-hour block of time. The birth time used is your local time, not adjusted to

Greenwich Mean Time as it would be by Western astrology. The only adjustment necessary is for births during Daylight Savings Time, which should not be used. Your birth time is called your *ascendant*, the sign that most colors your self-expression and how you respond to outside stimuli. Locate and record your birth time and the associated elemental information in chart 7, Elements of Birth Hour. At least two other systems exist that list different elements for the two-hour blocks of time. However, for our purposes, the most prevalent system of Chinese astrology is included in *Healing Design*. This system is taught by Theodora Lau, a leading authority on the subject, in her book, *The Handbook of Chinese Horoscopes*.

After the birth year and time, the birth month is considered. The twelve animals rule each of the months and correspond in time with the Western solar-based astrological system. Find your birth month on chart 8, Elements of Birth Month, and note the governing animal and its element.

The final section of this Five Element Configuration focuses on your birth country. A country's element is dictated by the date the country's government was formed or reformed. This can be difficult to calculate due to political upheavals. See chart 9, Elements of Birth Country.

Next, check to see whether all five elements are represented. Because there are only five lines and five elements, it is likely that some elements are not included in your chart. Most people discover that one, two, or even three elements are not present. (*Note:* If you have the four elements Water, Wood, Fire, and Metal, you are granted the fifth element, Earth, as the Earth is made up of the other four elements. Only the Earth element works in this way.) If you are missing an(y) element(s), include them in your home through colors, materials, and shapes as recommended in chart 2, The Five Elements.

Chart 1. The World of Yin/Yang: Achieving Balance

In Chinese cosmology, yin and yang are the two mutable, primordial forces that make up the universe. All phenomena can be categorized under these two opposing, yet complementary forces. Yin, or the feminine receptive principle in nature, is exhibited in darkness, cold, or wetness, and combines with yang to produce all that comes to be. Yang, or the masculine active principle in nature, is exhibited in light, heat, or dryness, and combines with yin to produce all that comes to be.

The paths of yin and yang energy are always in motion, moving toward one another in a spiraling dance, converging and changing into their opposite forms. Daytime is yang, bright and warm, but changes into yin, the cool, dark night. Whatever we observe in nature has a touch of the opposite energy, whether it be yin or yang. The bright yang day has dark yin shadows under the trees, whereas the dark yin night has the bright yang stars and moon.

When contemplating whether something is yin or yang, consider the big picture and how the item relates to the whole. For example, imagine the color red, which is normally considered a yang color. When we look at a deep, dark burgundy red or a diffuse mauve-rose, these darker shades project yin, while fire-engine red projects yang.

All things are relative! Resist the temptation to view anything individually or to perceive something as unconnected. Approach your decisions and choices as part of a higher path moving toward greater balance, comfort, and wholeness. Strive to unite yin and yang in an effort to experience the Tao, the fulcrum that is harmony—the balance of heaven and earth.

After locating information related to your birth in the charts in this chapter, an overall picture will emerge showing your personal yin/yang balance as well as your five element make-up. In feng shui, our goal is to create balance in our personal surroundings by bringing in more yin if most of our personal composition is yang, and vice versa. The same holds true for our personal formation involving the five elements. While we want to emphasize our natal and nourishing elements, we especially want to incorporate any of the elements missing from our personal charts.

To Increase Yin:

Spend more introspective, relaxing, solitary time. Pursue the spiritual, emotional, and intuitive, inner aspects of life. Work with ideas and imagination. *Yin represents one's innate capacity:* Cultivate this inner nature by focusing on feelings of *receptivity*, humility, and flexibility. Develop your inner essence. (Close relation-

Use cool colors: blue-greens; blues and purples; muted, diffuse colors; and dark shades. Use dimmed lighting and cool temperatures. Hang artwork and photography depicting heavenly themes and representations. Use curved lines in designs in the structure of the environment, your furnishings, and/or in patterns in fabric and artwork.

To Increase Yang:

Spend more time in outward-tending, ambitious, material pursuits. *Be active.* Cultivate your outer expression, organization, physical strength, and social interactions. Develop your intellectual side of life. Initiate projects. *Yang represents one's innate knowledge.*

Use warm colors: yellow-green, yellows, oranges, and reds. Use lighter, brighter, or intense colors, bright lighting, and warm temperatures. Hang artwork or photography depicting earthly representations, especially tall mountains. Use straight, angular, or rectilinear lines in designs, furnishings, or in patterns in fabric and artwork.

Chart 2. The Five Elements

In *Between Heaven and Earth*, acupuncturists and authors Harriet Beinfield and Efrem Korngold describe the five elements this way: "As a pair of reading glasses clarifies what is in front of our noses, these five patterns of movement bring into focus our relationships—our way of interacting with the world. As a telescope magnifies the constellations, this paradigm helps us grasp the vast scheme of the universe, aiding us in the divination of our certain place between heaven and earth."

To create a feeling of wholeness and to connect with all the aspects of nature in one's home, all five elements should ideally be represented in each room. So as not to dull the overall picture, however, emphasize one or two elements, accenting with the others. Often the most engaging designs are built around one or two predominant hues. The following passage from the *Tao Te Ching,* by Lao-Tzu speaks directly to the need for discerning choices.

The clarity in seeing is blinded by bright colors.

The sharpness of hearing is dulled by loud sounds.
The keenness of tasting is overcome by rich flavors.

Indulging the senses interferes with insight.
Precious things are distracting.

Therefore,

The sage is guided by the subtle, rather than the conspicuous;
By what is inside, rather than what is outside.*

After becoming familiar with your personal chart, use the five elements to highlight your nourishing and natal elements, or to bring about balance by supplementing any "missing elements." You might also want to consider giving a room some of its nourishing element. For example, a room oriented towards the south (Fire) is nourished by green, blue, and/or teal (Wood).

Because everything in the universe fits into the Five Element Theory, there are associations in all areas of our lives, and many ways for the five elements to provide support.

Wood: Yang. Directions: east, southeast. Colors: medium tones of blue, green, and teal, the colors most prevalent in foliage. Shape: tall pillar shapes, like columns. ▌▌ Lighting quality: clear and bright, like morning sunshine. We can bring more of the Wood element into our homes with wooden furniture, paneling, and flooring; striped fabric or fabric with floral or foliage designs; cotton or linen fabrics (made from plants); all plant life: bonsai, houseplants, flowers, window boxes, herb pots, trees, and dried flowers; bamboo flutes; picture frames; artwork and photos depicting trees or flowers; wood sculptures; columns and pedestals; furniture; lampshades; art and objects in the wood colors. Note that living vegetation—plants, trees, flowers, and herbs—has the strongest wood energy for one's home, stronger than wooden furniture, for example, that no longer lives and breathes as do live plants.

The emotional energies of the Wood element are creativity, vision, idealism, imagination, compassion, and determination. It assists in expansion of thought, initiative, and planning.

*Ray Grigg. *The New Lao Tzu: A Contemporary Tao te ching.* Boston: Tuttle, 1995.

The physical body areas ruled by Wood are the liver, gallbladder, and eyes. The archetype is the pioneer. The associated planet, Jupiter.

Fire: Extreme Yang. Direction: south. Colors: reds and pinks. Shapes: diagonal lines, pointed sharp angles like triangles or peaks. ▲ Lighting quality: warm, constant light; achieve this through lampshades of red and/or pink. We can bring more of the Fire element into our homes with candles, fireplaces, mirrors, night-lights, incense, goldfish, red or pink flowers, oil lamps, artwork or photos showing the sun, animals, silk and woolen fabrics (made from animal-originated fibers), and art, furniture, and objects ablaze with the fire colors.

The emotional energies of the Fire element are inspiration, passion, radiance, assertiveness, and awareness. It assists in realization, fulfillment, intuition, and intimacy.

The Fire element guards the heart and small intestines. The archetype is the wizard. The associated planet, Mars.

Earth: Yin. The point of balance. Directions: northeast, southwest, and the center of a space. Colors: copper, bronze, yellow, gold, orange, peach, salmon, beige, brown. Shapes: square or horizontal rectangles. ■ Lighting quality: rainbow; cut-crystal prisms or spheres hung in windows, crystal chandeliers, and crystal lampshades are a few methods to achieve prismatic lighting effects. Also consider lampshades in earth tones (see above) or that depict all of the colors of the rainbow together. We can bring more of the Earth element into our homes with ceramic pottery, bricks, concrete and concrete items, stones, terra-cotta, sand gardens, concrete items, houseplants (soil), brass ornaments (an earth tone), semiprecious stones, gemstone jewelry, fossils, artwork or photos of the earth, ceramic tile, ceramic drawer pulls and doorknobs, small carved stone sculptures, ceramic picture frames, and furniture or objects in earth tones.

The emotional energies of the Earth element are generosity, thoughtfulness, transformation, practicality, and stability. It assists in moderation, unification, and connectedness.

Physically, the Earth element governs the spleen, pancreas, and mouth. The archetype is the peacemaker. The associated planet, Saturn.

Metal: Yin. Directions: west, northwest. Colors: white and silver. Shapes: round or domed, like arches. ∩ ● Lighting quality: cool light. Metal lampshades or lampshades in white, off-white, or silver. We can bring more of the Metal element into our homes with wrought-iron furniture or candelabras, metal kitchen utensils, metal hardware on furniture and cabinets, brass ornaments, metal doorknobs, silver candleholders, silver and gold jewelry, metal sculpture, birdcages, planters and picture frames, decorative metalwork in fencing or garden decor, coins, coin collections (and all aspects of finances), brass or copper birdbaths, gongs, swords, electronics and computers (communication), and art or objects in the metal colors listed above.

The emotional energies of the Metal element are discipline, solidity, and fluency in speech. It assists in transmutation, organization, and mastery. In the physical body the Metal element rules the lungs, respiratory system, and the large intestine. The archetype is the alchemist. The associated planet, Venus.

Water: Extreme Yin. Direction: north. Colors: navy and black, the depth of water. Shapes: irregular, flowing and free form, just as water will take the shape of any vessel or crevice it fills. ♣ Lighting quality: reflected light, such as off a mirror or body of water. Lights through water, such as lighted water fountains, or through dark-colored lampshades, or glass lampshades, especially with wavy or rippled glass, achieve this lighting quality. We can bring the Water element into our homes with clear vases containing water and flowers, fishbowls, aquariums, fountains, water gardens, water dispensers, seashells, artwork or photos showing water; views through windows of a water fountain, waterfall, stream, pond, lake, or ocean; furniture; and objects or art in which the colors navy or black predominate.

The emotional energies of the Water element are willpower, magnetism, sensitivity, wisdom, persuasiveness, and the ability to focus the mind. It assists in consolidation, revelation, and knowledge.

The kidneys, bladder, and ears are ruled by the Water element. Its archetype is the philosopher. The associated planet, Mercury.

Chart 3. Yearly Elements

This chart holds a wealth of information. It is based on the Chinese system of a lunar year, which starts with the second New Moon following the Winter

Solstice. The Chinese day begins at 11 P.M. instead of 12 A.M., so if you were born between 11 P.M. and midnight, your date of birth falls on the following day in this system. Your birth year information holds the key to the most prominent aspects of your character

Time Span	Year's Energy	Ten Heavenly Stems Year's Element	Twelve Earthly Branches Animal sign	Pa-Kua Number Male	Female
Jan 31, 1900 to Feb 18, 1901	Yang	Metal	Rat	1	5
Feb 19, 1901 to Feb 7, 1902	Yin	Metal	Ox	9	6
Feb 8, 1902 to Jan 28, 1903	Yang	Water	Tiger	8	7
Jan 29, 1903 to Feb 15, 1904	Yin	Water	Rabbit	7	8
Feb 16, 1904 to Feb 3, 1905	Yang	Wood	Dragon	6	9
Feb 4, 1905 to Jan 24, 1906	Yin	Wood	Snake	5	1
Jan 25, 1906 to Feb 12, 1907	Yang	Fire	Horse	4	2
Feb 13, 1907 to Feb 1, 1908	Yin	Fire	Sheep	3	3
Feb 2, 1908 to Jan 21, 1909	Yang	Earth	Monkey	2	4
Jan 22, 1909 to Feb 9, 1910	Yin	Earth	Rooster	1	5
Feb 10, 1910 to Jan 29, 1911	Yang	Metal	Dog	9	6
Jan 30, 1911 to Feb 17, 1912	Yin	Metal	Boar	8	7
Feb 18, 1912 to Feb 5, 1913	Yang	Water	Rat	7	8
Feb 6, 1913 to Jan 25, 1914	Yin	Water	Ox	6	9
Jan 26, 1914 to Feb 13, 1915	Yang	Wood	Tiger	5	1
Feb 14, 1915 to Feb 2, 1916	Yin	Wood	Rabbit	4	2
Feb 3, 1916 to Jan 22, 1917	Yang	Fire	Dragon	3	3
Jan 23, 1917 to Feb 10, 1918	Yin	Fire	Snake	2	4
Feb 11, 1918 to Jan 31, 1919	Yang	Earth	Horse	1	5
Feb 1, 1919 to Feb 19, 1920	Yin	Earth	Sheep	9	6
Feb 20, 1920 to Feb 7, 1921	Yang	Metal	Monkey	8	7
Feb 8, 1921 to Jan 27, 1922	Yin	Metal	Rooster	7	8
Jan 28, 1922 to Feb 15, 1923	Yang	Water	Dog	6	9
Feb 16, 1923 to Feb 4, 1924	Yin	Water	Boar	5	1

Time Span	Year's Energy	Year's Element	Animal sign	Male	Female
Feb 5, 1924 to Jan 24, 1925	Yang	Wood	Rat	4	2
Jan 25, 1925 to Feb 12, 1926	Yin	Wood	Ox	3	3
Feb 13, 1926 to Feb 1, 1927	Yang	Fire	Tiger	2	4
Feb 2, 1927 to Jan 22, 1928	Yin	Fire	Rabbit	1	5
Jan 23, 1928 to Feb 9, 1929	Yang	Earth	Dragon	9	6
Feb 10, 1929 to Jan 29, 1930	Yin	Earth	Snake	8	7
Jan 30, 1930 to Feb 16, 1931	Yang	Metal	Horse	7	8
Feb 17, 1931 to Feb 5, 1932	Yin	Metal	Sheep	6	9
Feb 6, 1932 to Jan 25, 1933	Yang	Water	Monkey	5	1
Jan 26, 1933 to Feb 13, 1934	Yin	Water	Rooster	4	2
Feb 14, 1934 to Feb 3, 1935	Yang	Wood	Dog	3	3
Feb 4, 1935 to Jan 23, 1936	Yin	Wood	Boar	2	4
Jan 24, 1936 to Feb 10, 1937	Yang	Fire	Rat	1	5
Feb 11, 1937 to Jan 30, 1938	Yin	Fire	Ox	9	6
Jan 31, 1938 to Feb 18, 1939	Yang	Earth	Tiger	8	7
Feb 19, 1939 to Feb 7, 1940	Yin	Earth	Rabbit	7	8
Feb 8, 1940 to Jan 26, 1941	Yang	Metal	Dragon	6	9
Jan 27, 1941 to Feb 14, 1942	Yin	Metal	Snake	5	1
Feb 15, 1942 to Feb 4, 1943	Yang	Water	Horse	4	2
Feb 5, 1943 to Jan 24, 1944	Yin	Water	Sheep	3	3
Jan 25, 1944 to Feb 12, 1945	Yang	Wood	Monkey	2	4
Feb 13, 1945 to Feb 1, 1946	Yin	Wood	Rooster	1	5
Feb 2, 1946 to Jan 21, 1947	Yang	Fire	Dog	9	6
Jan 22, 1947 to Feb 9, 1948	Yin	Fire	Boar	8	7
Feb 10, 1948 to Jan 28, 1949	Yang	Earth	Rat	7	8
Jan 29, 1949 to Feb 16, 1950	Yin	Earth	Ox	6	9
Feb 17, 1950 to Feb 5, 1951	Yang	Metal	Tiger	5	1
Feb 6, 1951 to Jan 26, 1952	Yin	Metal	Rabbit	4	2
Jan 27, 1952 to Feb 13, 1953	Yang	Water	Dragon	3	3
Feb 14, 1953 to Feb 2, 1954	Yin	Water	Snake	2	4
Feb 3, 1954 to Jan 23, 1955	Yang	Wood	Horse	1	5

Time Span	Year's Energy	Year's Element	Animal sign	Male	Female
Jan 24, 1955 to Feb 11, 1956	Yin	Wood	Sheep	9	6
Feb 12, 1956 to Jan 30, 1957	Yang	Fire	Monkey	8	7
Jan 31, 1957 to Feb 17, 1958	Yin	Fire	Rooster	7	8
Feb 18, 1958 to Feb 7, 1959	Yang	Earth	Dog	6	9
Feb 8, 1959 to Jan 27, 1960	Yin	Earth	Boar	5	1
Jan 28, 1960 to Feb 14, 1961	Yang	Metal	Rat	4	2
Feb 15, 1961 to Feb 4, 1962	Yin	Metal	Ox	3	3
Feb 5, 1962 to Jan 24, 1963	Yang	Water	Tiger	2	4
Jan 25, 1963 to Feb 12, 1964	Yin	Water	Rabbit	1	5
Feb 13, 1964 to Feb 1, 1965	Yang	Wood	Dragon	9	6
Feb 2, 1965 to Jan 20, 1966	Yin	Wood	Snake	8	7
Jan 21, 1966 to Feb 8, 1967	Yang	Fire	Horse	7	8
Feb 9, 1967 to Jan 29, 1968	Yin	Fire	Sheep	6	9
Jan 30, 1968 to Feb 16, 1969	Yang	Earth	Monkey	5	1
Feb 17, 1969 to Feb 5, 1970	Yin	Earth	Rooster	4	2
Feb 6, 1970 to Jan 26, 1971	Yang	Metal	Dog	3	3
Jan 27, 1971 to Feb 15, 1972	Yin	Metal	Boar	2	4
Feb 16, 1972 to Feb 2, 1973	Yang	Water	Rat	1	5
Feb 3, 1973 to Jan 22, 1974	Yin	Water	Ox	9	6
Jan 23, 1974 to Feb 10, 1975	Yang	Wood	Tiger	8	7
Feb 11, 1975 to Jan 30, 1976	Yin	Wood	Rabbit	7	8
Jan 31, 1976 to Feb 17, 1977	Yang	Fire	Dragon	6	9
Feb 18, 1977 to Feb 6, 1978	Yin	Fire	Snake	5	1
Feb 7, 1978 to Jan 27, 1979	Yang	Earth	Horse	4	2
Jan 28, 1979 to Feb 15, 1980	Yin	Earth	Sheep	3	3
Feb 16, 1980 to Feb 4, 1981	Yang	Metal	Monkey	2	4
Feb 5, 1981 to Jan 24, 1982	Yin	Metal	Rooster	1	5
Jan 25, 1982 to Feb 12, 1983	Yang	Water	Dog	9	6
Feb 13, 1983 to Feb 1, 1984	Yin	Water	Boar	8	7
Feb 2, 1984 to Feb 19, 1985	Yang	Wood	Rat	7	8
Feb 20, 1985 to Feb 8, 1986	Yin	Wood	Ox	6	9

Time Span	Year's Energy	Year's Element	Animal sign	Male	Female
Feb 9, 1986 to Jan 28, 1987	Yang	Fire	Tiger	5	1
Jan 29, 1987 to Feb 16, 1988	Yin	Fire	Rabbit	4	2
Feb 17, 1988 to Feb 5, 1989	Yang	Earth	Dragon	3	3
Feb 6, 1989 to Jan 26, 1990	Yin	Earth	Snake	2	4
Jan 27, 1990 to Feb 14, 1991	Yang	Metal	Horse	1	5
Feb 15, 1991 to Feb 3, 1992	Yin	Metal	Sheep	9	6
Feb 4, 1992 to Jan 22, 1993	Yang	Water	Monkey	8	7
Jan 23, 1993 to Feb 9, 1994	Yin	Water	Rooster	7	8
Feb 10, 1994 to Jan 30, 1995	Yang	Wood	Dog	6	9
Jan 31, 1995 to Feb 18, 1996	Yin	Wood	Boar	5	1
Feb 19, 1996 to Feb 6, 1997	Yang	Fire	Rat	4	2
Feb 7, 1997 to Jan 27, 1998	Yin	Fire	Ox	3	3
Jan 28, 1998 to Feb 15, 1999	Yang	Earth	Tiger	2	4
Feb 16, 1999 to Feb 4, 2000	Yin	Earth	Rabbit	1	5
Feb 5, 2000 to Jan 23, 2001	Yang	Metal	Dragon	9	6
Jan 24, 2001 to Feb 11, 2002	Yin	Metal	Snake	8	7
Feb 12, 2002 to Jan 31, 2003	Yang	Water	Horse	7	8
Feb 1, 2003 to Jan 21, 2004	Yin	Water	Sheep	6	9
Jan 22, 2004 to Feb 8, 2005	Yang	Wood	Monkey	5	1
Feb 9, 2005 to Jan 28, 2006	Yin	Wood	Rooster	4	2
Jan 29, 2006 to Feb 17, 2007	Yang	Fire	Dog	3	3
Feb 18, 2007 to Feb 6, 2008	Yin	Fire	Boar	2	4

Chart 4. Compass Directions for Each Kua

The following information comes from the teachings and translations of Lillian Too as presented in her book *Applied Pa-Kua and Lo Shu Feng Shui*. Ms. Too holds an MBA from Harvard and was the first female bank president in Hong Kong. After personally discovering the relevance of feng shui, she began translating the works of two masters in her many books on the subject.

This compass school information suggests that, based on one's birth year, there are four fortunate directions to tap into for each individual. Locate your personal pa-kua number in the far right column of chart 3. See this chart for your pa-kua number's best four directions. The most important use of this information relates to the direction your front door faces when measured from inside the door looking out, the wall in your bedroom against which you place your headboard, and the direction your body faces when sitting at your desk or in your favorite easy chair, anywhere you spend a fair amount of time. These best four directions may be used to your advantage when giving a speech or when being interviewed for new employment. Angle your body to one of your most fortunate directions.

Pa-Kua Number	Best Direction	Second Best Direction	Third Best Direction	Fourth Best Direction	Fourth Worst Direction	Third Worst Direction	Second Worst Direction	Worst Direction
1	SE	E	S	N	W	NE	NW	SW
2	NE	W	NW	SW	E	SE	S	N
3	S	N	SE	E	SW	NW	NE	W
4	N	S	E	SE	NW	SW	W	NE
5 (male)	NE	W	NW	SW	E	SE	S	N
5 (female)	SW	NW	W	NE	S	N	E	SE
6	W	NE	SW	NW	SE	E	N	S
7	NW	SW	NE	W	N	S	SE	E
8	SW	NW	W	NE	S	N	E	SE
9	E	SE	N	S	NE	W	SW	NW

Chart 5. Birth Months and Natal Element

In Chinese astrology, the months begin on different days each year. This originated with the movement of the sun in an agricultural calendar. (For concise information on the division of months from year to year, see Evelyn Lip's book, *Personalize Your Feng Shui*.)

You will now use your pa-kua number from chart 3 and follow down the appropriate column, male or female, under your pa-kua number until you reach the line for your birthdate. This is your natal element, your core essence. If your birthday falls on the cusp between two months, you may have to consider two possible natal elements, each having its own nourishing element. This gives you three or four elements to consider, depending on whether there is any overlap of elements. It is somewhat tricky, but as you work with the charts, your understanding will improve.

Pa-Kua Number

1	2	3
4	5	6
7	8	9

Approximate Division of Solar Months	Female	Male	Female	Male	Female	Male
Jan 5–7 to Feb 4–5	Yin Fire	Yang Metal	Yang Metal	Yin Fire	Yang Wood	Yang Wood
Feb 4–5 to Mar 5–7	Yin Metal	Yang Earth	Yin Wood	Yin Earth	Yang Water	Yang Earth
Mar 5–7 to Apr 4–6	Yang Earth	Yin Metal	Yin Earth	Yang Water	Yin Earth	Yin Wood
Apr 4–6 to May 5–7	Yin Fire	Yang Metal	Yang Metal	Yin Fire	Yang Wood	Yang Wood
May 5–7 to June 5–7	Yang Water	Yang Earth	Yin Metal	Yang Earth	Yin Wood	Yin Earth
June 5–7 to July 7–8	Yin Earth	Yin Wood	Yang Earth	Yin Metal	Yin Earth	Yang Water
July 7–8 to Aug 7–9	Yang Wood	Yang Wood	Yin Fire	Yang Metal	Yang Metal	Yin Fire
Aug 7–9 to Sept 7–9	Yang Wood	Yin Earth	Yang Water	Yang Earth	Yin Metal	Yang Earth
Sept 7–9 to Oct 8–9	Yin Earth	Yang Water	Yin Earth	Yin Wood	Yang Earth	Yin Metal
Oct 8–9 to Nov 7–8	Yang Metal	Yin Fire	Yang Wood	Yang Wood	Yin Fire	Yang Metal
Nov 7–8 to Dec 7–8	Yin Metal	Yang Earth	Yin Wood	Yin Earth	Yang Water	Yang Earth
Dec 7–8 to Jan 5–7	Yang Earth	Yin Metal	Yin Earth	Yang Water	Yin Earth	Yin Wood

Chart 6. Natural Elements of the Twelve Animal Signs

There are many animals in your individual "totem." Many indigenous cultures, while believing in a single supreme deity, acknowledge the metaphors of the energy and patterns of animals. This helps to understand one's place in the animated world through the metaphor of the animal. Each animal is an allegory for numerous personal qualities. In addition to the animal that rules your birth year, others represent the time, month, and location of your birth. Each animal affects and tempers the others, creating a fun, interesting way of adding to your self-knowledge

Animal	Natural Element of Animal	Description
Rat	Yang Water	Sentimental, devoted, resourceful, protective, energetic, persistent, insightful, charming, clever, and loving. May seem outwardly shy but inwardly is competitive and ambitious. Take care not to spend money too freely. Suitable careers are in any capacity of business: retail store owner, banker, accountant, or writer.
Ox	Yin Water	Works hard and methodically. Strong-willed. Enjoys helping others and often inspires others. Original, receptive, steadfast, eloquent, bright, and capable. Cautioned against being stubborn or overly authoritarian. Do well in career as architect, tailor, dentist, surgeon, hairdresser, or mechanic.
Tiger	Yang Wood	Courageous, active, and self-assured. Candid, magnetic, sensitive, independent, versatile, and unpredictable. Guard against being restless or impulsive. Tiger personalities are especially suited to become supervisors, politicians, teachers, chefs, leaders in any branch of the armed forces, police officers, or firefighters.
Rabbit	Yin Wood	Quick, clever, ambitious, lucky, tactful, refined, talented, and articulate. Affectionate and social, yet shy. You seek peace throughout your life. Sensitive and finely tuned. Can be restless and impatient, so take care to finish what you start. Careers include interior design, publicist, pharmacist, stockbroker, beautician, massage therapist, or receptionist.
Dragon	Yang Wood	Considered in China to be the most desirable year to be born. Dynamic, complex, determined, eccentric, confident, healthy, full of vitality and creativity. Also possesses a mystical side: intuitive, artistic, and strangely lucky. Guard against irritability and stubbornness. A dragon will live well as an artist, doctor, politician, architect, actor, or in the clergy.
Snake	Yin Fire	Sometimes called "the little dragon." Full of ideas. Thoughtful, philosophical, intuitive, independent, calm, and understanding. Sophisticated, wise, passionate, and intense. Guard against being lazy, vain, or vengeful. Snake personalities make wonderful teachers, writers, philosophers, politicians, or therapists.

Animal	Natural Element of Animal	Description
Horse	Yang Fire	Charming and cheerful. Popular, outgoing, and extremely likable. Hard working, sharp, persuasive, dashing, and ambitious. Guard against being too frank, obstinate, or impatient. Those born in the year of the horse do well as an architect, dentist, chemist, banker, diplomat, doctor, or politician.
Sheep	Yin Fire	Good natured, peaceloving, humanitarian, inventive, and whimsical, finely tuned, elegant aesthetics. Innate intelligence and creative, artistic talent. Take care against being wishy-washy, undisciplined, or fretful. Sometimes timid, preferring anonymity. Those born in sheep years are known for excellence in the fields of public entertaining, painting, music, photography, acting, and gardening. Generally fares well in business.
Monkey	Yang Metal	Enthusiastic, ingenious, amusing, and witty. Inventive. Can solve problems well and quickly, accomplishes much in business, very intelligent and versatile. Are able to influence people. Guard against being lazy or discouraged. Don't focus on small points while ignoring the overall picture. One born in the year of the monkey easily finds success in any aspect of business: the stock market, law, diplomacy, or politics.
Rooster	Yin Metal	Hardworking, meticulous, resourceful, talented, and self-assured. Courageous, logical, practical, and enduring. A pioneer in spirit, in a quest after knowledge. Take care not to be pedantic or boastful. Roosters find fame and good fortune when involved in any area of travel or public relations. Careers include hair stylist, dentist, surgeon, chef, or restaurant manager.
Dog	Yang Metal	Faithful, trusting, and honest. A courageous friend. Deep sense of justice, security, and guardianship, especially for family and friends. Inspires confidence in people. This sign accomplishes goals quickly, being quite persevering and intelligent. Take care against being defensive or pessimistic. Careers to consider are the clergy, education, doctor, supervisor, writer, scientist, or business leader.
Boar	Yin Water	Sincere, loving, thorough, chivalrous, and courageous. Intelligent, social, and congenial. On the surface, may seem jovial; inside is pure gold: natural and nice. May need to work to harmonize marriage relationships. Guard against being too naive or defenseless. Boars make excellent doctors, bankers, scientists, manufacturers, entertainers, and are good in many aspects of business.

Chart 7. Elements of Birth Hour

The animal and element of your birth time (not adjusted to Daylight Savings Time) strongly influence your self-expression and how others see you, even your physical appearance. They also give insight into how you respond to stimuli.

Time	Natural Element	Ruling Animal
11 P.M. to 1 A.M.	Yang Water	Rat
1 A.M. to 3 A.M.	Yin Water	Ox
3 A.M. to 5 A.M.	Yang Wood	Tiger
5 A.M. to 7 A.M.	Yin Wood	Rabbit
7 A.M. to 9 A.M.	Yang Wood	Dragon
9 A.M. to 11 A.M.	Yin Fire	Snake
11 A.M. to 1 P.M.	Yang Fire	Horse
1 P.M. to 3 P.M.	Yin Fire	Sheep
3 P.M. to 5 P.M.	Yang Metal	Monkey
5 P.M. to 7 P.M.	Yin Metal	Rooster
7 P.M. to 9 P.M.	Yang Metal	Dog
9 P.M. to 11 P.M.	Yin Water	Boar

Chart 8. Elements of Birth Month

In Asian astrology, each of the twelve animals governs a month. These dates match the Western solar signs. If your birthday is between the 18th and 23rd of a month, you are born on the cusp and may have some personality influences from both signs. The month of birth applies to the emotional and creative energy of an individual.

Month	Natural Element	Astrological Sign	Ruling Animal
January 20 to February 18	Yang Wood	Aquarius	Tiger
February 19 to March 20	Yin Wood	Pisces	Rabbit
March 21 to April 19	Yang Wood	Aries	Dragon
April 20 to May 20	Yin Fire	Taurus	Snake

Month	Natural Element	Astrological Sign	Ruling Animal
May 21 to June 21	Yang Fire	Gemini	Horse
June 22 to July 22	Yin Fire	Cancer	Sheep
July 23 to August 22	Yang Metal	Leo	Monkey
August 23 to September 22	Yin Metal	Virgo	Rooster
September 23 to October 23	Yang Metal	Libra	Dog
October 24 to November 22	Yin Water	Scorpio	Boar
November 23 to December 21	Yang Water	Sagittarius	Rat
December 22 to January 19	Yin Water	Capricorn	Ox

Chart 9. Elements of Birth Country

The element governing a country depends on the year the country's government came into being. This is sometimes difficult to establish, particularly in turbulent times when regimes change. Each time a country comes under new rule, not just a new leader, but an entirely different government, the ruling animal and element change as well. If not listed below, determine the governing element of the country you were born in by starting with your birth year. Find out what government was in rule during your birth year and which year it came into power. Look up the year the reigning government came into power in chart 3. While the element and governing animal of your birthplace do not have as much impact on your daily life as the rest of your feng shui chart, one's culture definitely has influential effects. This can be experienced when recognizing that subtle similarity you may feel upon meeting someone from your own country when you are traveling in a foreign nation.

Country	Natal Element	Ruling Animal	Year
Australia	Yin Metal	Ox	
Canada	Yin Fire	Rabbit	
China	Yin Fire	Ox	
Cuba	Yang Water	Tiger	
England	Yin Earth	Sheep	

Country	Natal Element	Ruling Animal	Year*
France	Yang Earth	Dog	
Germany	Yin Metal	Sheep	Until mid-1949
	Yin Earth	Ox	mid-1949 to present
Hong Kong	Yin Metal	Tiger	Before 1997
	Yin Fire	Ox	June 30, 1997 and forward
India	Yin Fire	Boar	Since August 15, 1947
Israel	Yang Earth	Rat	
Italy	Yang Water	Dog	1922 to September 1945
	Yin Wood	Rooster	September 1945 to present
Japan	Yin Earth	Ox	1889 to 1946
	Yin Fire	Boar	1947 to present
Kenya, Africa	Yang Metal	Monkey	
New Zealand	Yin Fire	Sheep	1907 to 1947
	Yin Fire	Boar	1947 to present
Pakistan	Yin Fire	Boar	
Philippines	Yang Fire	Dog	
Russia†	Yin Fire	Snake	
United States	Yang Metal	Monkey	
Vietnam	Yang Wood	Horse	

* Years are given only for countries whose governments have changed.
† After the social changes of the early 1990s, the fifteen Soviet Republics became independent; each should be categorized according to the date their new governing bodies took effect.

Sample Chart: Luciano Pavarotti

Born October 12, 1935, 2 A.M., Modena, Italy

The Five Element Configuration

Year of birth:	Yin Wood Boar
Natural element of your animal sign:	Yin Water
Element of your birth hour:	Yin Water
Element of your birth month:	Yang Metal
Element of your birth country:	Yang Water

Pa-Kua Number:	2
Compass directions listed from best to worst:	NE, W, NW, SW, E, SE, S, N
Natal Element:	Yang Wood
Nourishing Element:	Water (precedes Wood in the nourishing cycle)

Mr. Pavarotti has both yin and yang energy represented in his Five Element Configuration—a nice balance that requires no additional compensation from his environment in order to create harmony in the receptive/active levels of life.

Born in the year of the Yin Wood Boar and with Wood as his natal element, a great quantity of the Wood element energies are present in his life. This manifests as expanded creativity, optimism, and good humor, creating an abundant, satisfying life. Many people are not happy to learn they are born under the Year of the Boar, or pig. The other sign that many scoff at being born under is the rat. Every animal year has its positive and shadow aspects. The different animal years simply describe various qualities of energy and emotional and personality attributes.

Being born under the Year of the Boar, Mr. Pavarotti is an excellent conversationalist and very popular. Boars are especially reliable, generous, and social. They enjoy helping others and love to entertain, as Mr. Pavarotti has in his numerous concerts throughout the years.

Mr. Pavarotti's entire chart shows that his energetic make-up consists totally of Wood (vision, creativity), Water (depth, emotion), and Metal (connecting, communicating). This is exactly how his career is playing out; he creatively connects and communicates about the emotional realms of life through his performance of opera.

The remaining two elements, Earth and Fire, when brought into his surroundings, will augment feelings of wholeness and support. The Earth element, through colors, shapes, or materials, increases the feeling of groundedness and stability of being centered. Touches of the Fire element impart additional inspiration and focus to Mr. Pavarotti's life and help replenish all of the passion he infuses into his music.

Chart 10. The Magic Measurements in Feng Shui

For centuries, in both the East and West, there have been schools of thought related to both the practical and spiritual significance of numbers and measurements. In the Western body of mathematics, the square root of two is called the *golden section*. This unit of measure is found in examining many aspects of nature, including flowers, seashells, and the human body.

This same ratio, the measurement of the diagonal of a square Chinese foot (the Chinese foot being about 17 inches [43 cm]), has long been thought to have mystical, spiritual significance. In two Chinese systems, the 17 inches is divided into either ten or eight sections. The eight-section division is used in feng shui measurements.

The dimensions related to beneficial, auspicious results are applied in the design of furniture, homes, and practical items such as briefcases to influence, whenever possible, the support of one's good fortune and luck by being more in sync with the magical, mystical aspects of life.

For measurements larger than 17 inches, deduct as many full increments of 17 inches as possible, and compare the remaining portion to the following chart.

Measurement	Symbolism	Chinese Name
0 to 2 1/8" (5.4 cm)	Wealth	Ts'ai
2 3/16" to 4 1/4" (10.7 cm)	Sickness	Ping
4 5/16" to 6 5/16" (16.1 cm)	Separation	Li
6 3/8" to 8 7/16" (21.4 cm)	Righteousness	I
8 1/2" to 10 1/2" (26.8 cm)	Promotion	Kuan
10 5/8" to 12 5/8" (32.1 cm)	Robbery	Chieh
12 3/4" to 14 3/4" (37.5 cm)	Accident	Hai
14 13/16" to 16 15/16" (42.9 cm)	Source	Pen

Note: The feng shui foot (17" or any increment of 17" [43 cm]) is considered auspicious, as the number borders the categories of source and wealth.

Chart 11. Symbolism

Much understanding can be gained by embracing the symbolism of various cultures. Symbols speak to conscious, subconscious, and superconscious levels in a universal language, offering an immediate way of communicating with ourselves and others. For your home to speak to your spirit, be sure to include abundant personal symbolism.

Color	Meaning
Black	Hidden, mysterious. The positive association is water and money, the negative lack of light. Not to be overused; can be vacuous. Water element.
Blue	The sky and space; sometimes its coolness connotes death. Wood element.
Brown	Fertile; that from which beauty can grow. Earth element.
Gold	Wealth, the sun, illumination; one of the two luckiest colors. Earth element. Shiny gold is Metal element.
Green	Tranquility, healing, balance, growth, spring, and freshness. Wood element.
Orange	Active and creative. Earth element.
Pink	Marriage, universal love, joy. Pink combines red (Fire element) and white (Metal element).
Purple	Wealth, regal, the fusion of red (yang) and blue (yin). Highest vibration of visible spectrum. Some shades represent the Water element. Purple combines blue (Wood element) and red (Fire element).
Red	Festivity, happiness, joy, passion; one of the two luckiest colors. The most physical, active color. Fire element.
White	The positive association is purity, the negative mourning and death. Metal element.
Yellow	Longevity; represents the sun. Earth element.

Animal symbol	Meaning
Bat	Prosperity/luck
Bear	Strength/yang energy; also protective mother instincts
Bird	Thought/imagination/freedom
Butterfly	Transformation/the soul
Cat	Personal pride/love of comfort
Cicada	Life after death
Crane	Longevity/lifelong marriage
Deer	Wealth/maternal affection/healing touch
Dog	Companionship/household guardian

Animal symbol	Meaning
Dolphin	Connection between human consciousness and the animal kingdom
Dove	Peace/love
Dragon	Yang power/spiritualization of earthly substances/life-force energies coursing through land forms
Eagle	Strength; eagle feathers are light on one side, dark on the other, representing substance and shadow
Elephant	Strength/wisdom/good luck when trunk is extended upward
Fish	Success/fertility/riches
Fox	Clever
Horse	Great power with gentility
Lion	Strength; the raw power of the Fire element
Peacock	Beauty; the male is connected to the clouds and rain
Phoenix	Yin power/resurrection/rising from the flames/immortality
Phoenix & Dragon	Yin/yang balance
Pig	Wealth (hence, piggy banks)
Rabbit	Fertility/abundance
Rooster	Reliability
Snake	Skill/transcendence/mediator; coiling represents the spiral of life
Stork	Ancient symbol of life
Swan	Feminine grace/beauty/divine inspiration
Tiger	Courage/protection
Toad	The Earth/instinct; recognizing beauty in homely things
Tortoise	Longevity/protective security
Unicorn	Wisdom/purity/innocence
Wolf	Inner, wild primitive level of being

Plant/Tree	Meaning
Acacia	Stability
Acorn	Future potential
Apple	Choices in life
Ash	Wisdom
Aster	Love
Azalea	Creativity
Bamboo	Longevity/youth/openness/flexibility

Plant/Tree	Meaning
Cedar	Immortality
Cherry	Good education
Chrysanthemum	Autumn
Chrysanthemum White	Truth
Cypress	Longevity/royalty/purity
Dogwood	Gentleness/harmony
Evergreen	Eternal life/immortality
Flowers (in general)	Wealth
Four Leaf Clover	Health/wealth/happiness/true love
Holly	Friendship/regeneration
Iris	Spring/the eye of heaven
Lily	Feminine purity
Loquat	Luck/wealth
Jasmine	Friendship
Juniper	Protection
Lotus	Endurance/uprightness/resurrection/fertility/spirit/creativity
Narcissus	Rejuvenation
Oak	Hospitality/endurance
Orange	Generosity/a gift of 12 oranges at the Chinese New Year invites happiness and prosperity
Orchid	Endurance/refinement/love and beauty
Peach	Longevity/friendship/charm/soul substance
Pear	Longevity/comfort
Peony	Summer/wealth/healing/protection/yang/happy marriage
Pine	Longevity/endurance/life force
Plum	Endurance/fidelity/beauty/youth
Pomegranate	Fertility/feminine
Poplar	Two-color leaf represents yin/yang
Rhododendron	Creativity
Rose	Beauty/emblem of the soul/love
Rose Pink	Perfect happiness
Rose Red	Love
Rose White	Purity

Plant/Tree	Meaning
Stephanotis	Happiness in marriage
Tangerine	Wealth
Trees (in general)	Ability to reach toward heaven while having roots in the earth
Walnut	Intellect
Willow	Grace/mourning/creativity
Yew	Strength/connection to god–goddess
Zinnia	Lasting affection

Nature	Meaning
Cloud	Spiritual quality/wisdom/heavenly blessing
Lightning	Striking swiftness of thought or action
Moon	Supreme yin/feminine mysteries/unconscious mind
Rain	Union (yin yang)
Sun	Spring/beginning/supreme yang/life source/conscious mind/intellect
Sun, rising	Confidence
Sun, setting	Downward trend
Shell	Water element/love/female sexuality
Water ripples	Wealth/heavenly blessing
Wind	Movement

Shape/Pattern	Meaning
Cross	Vertical line symbolizes infinity/spirit; horizontal line symbolizes finite consciousness
Feathers	Wealth/whisking away negativity
Fish scales	Success
Floral	Symmetry/Wood element/wealth
I Ching Trigram	Mythical power
Octagon	Luckiest shape/balance between movement and stability/heaven and earth
Oval	Sensuality, romantic bliss
Rectangle	Heavenly blessing/completeness/Earth element
Shell, conch	Sound to summon spirit
Shell, scallop	Femininity
Spiral	The ascending and descending movement of energy

Shape/Pattern	Meaning
Square	Stability/earthly blessing/Earth element
Straight Line	Movement in time and space
Triangle	Dynamic movement/trinity/Fire element
Tortoise shell	Longevity
Zigzag	Movement/Water element

Object	Meaning
Gold pieces	Wealth
Old coins	Wealth
Vase	Peace

Numbers	Meaning
Odd numbers	Yang
Even numbers	Yin
One	Unity; The Tao
Two	Yin/yang; duality
Three	Creativity, movement
Four	Thought to bring bad luck in East; in West, represents a foundation, stability
Five	Auspicious; The Five Elements
Six	Attracts wealth
Seven	In the Vedic system, represents the major energy spirals (chakras) of the body
Eight	Very auspicious; the infinity sign turned upright; represents bringing spirit down into matter; wealth and success; the Eight Trigrams of the *I Ching*, the Eight Immortals (revered Gods)
Nine	Most fortunate number in feng shui; wholeness, completion, altruism
Ten	The Ten Heavenly Stems; the yin and yang aspects of the Five Elements
Twelve	Chinese view of the hours in a day; the number of double hours, the twelve animal signs of the zodiac, the twelve earthly branches
Twenty-four	The segments of the Chinese solar calendar
Twenty-eight	The constellations of the Chinese lunar calendar
Sixty-four	The number of discourses in the *I Ching*; a 5000-year-old book of Chinese divination
Eighty-one	The chapters of the *Tao Te Ching*, an eminent book of Taoist wisdom

To deepen learning, I believe in focusing on one system of feng shui at a time. *Healing Design* primarily discusses the Black Hat Tantric Tibetan school of feng shui, which always orients the ba-gua to the entrance. Other systems of feng shui arrange the life positions according to compass orientations: Career/Life Journey is north, General Knowledge/Wisdom is northeast, Family/Health is east, Wealth is southeast, Fame/Advancement is south, Romantic Relationship/Marriage is southwest, Children/Creativity is west, and Travel/Helpful People is northwest. I use the compass to look at the overall five-element energy of a room and the Black Hat School to place symbolic items in a home.

Many important forms of feng shui (Four Pillars, Flying Star, Seven Portents, Lo Shu, Nine-Star-Ki) are included in the books listed in the bibliography. All of these ancient learnings and the breadth and depth to this art and science hold value and wisdom. Every book you read on the subject reveals additional facets of the spirit behind this form of design. It is truly a Magical Mystery Tour.

My best wishes for love and grace as you craft your home to nourish your soul and spirit.

Suggested Reading

General Reference

Day, Christopher. *Places of the Soul.* San Francisco: Aquarian Press, 1993.

Lin, Jami. *Contemporary Earth Design.* Miami Shores, Fl.: Earth Design, 1997.

Rossbach, Sarah. *Interior Design with Feng Shui.* New York: Viking Penguin, 1987.

Sang, Larry (Master). *The Principles of Feng Shui.* Monterey Park, Calif.: American Feng Shui Institute, 1994.

Spear, William. *Feng Shui Made Easy.* New York: HarperCollins, 1995.

Too, Lillian. *The Complete Illustrated Guide to Feng Shui.* Rockport, Mass.: Element Books, 1996.

Walters, Derek. *The Feng Shui Handbook.* San Francisco: Thorsons, 1991.

Spiritual Rituals and Color Analysis

Rossbach, Sarah, and Master Lin Yun. *Living Color.* New York: Kodansha America, 1994.

Feng Shui Cures

Collins, Terah Kathryn. *The Western Guide to Feng Shui.* Carlsbad, Calif.: Hay House, 1996.

Wydra, Nancilee. *Feng Shui: The Book of Cures.* Chicago: Contemporary Books, 1996.

Chinese Astrology

Lau, Theodora. *The Handbook of Chinese Horoscopes.* New York: HarperCollins, 1995.

Lip, Evelyn. *Personalize Your Feng Shui.* Torrance, Calif.: Heian International, 1997.

Sandifer, Jon. *Feng Shui Astrology.* New York: Ballantine, 1997.

Too, Lillian. *Applied Pa-Kua and Lo Shu Feng Shui.* Kuala Lumpur: Konsep Books, 1993.

White, Suzanne. *Suzanne White's Original Chinese Astrology Book.* Boston: Tuttle, 1990.

Wong, Eva. *Feng Shui: The Ancient Wisdom of Harmonious Living for Modern Times.* Boston: Shambhala, 1996.

Five Element Reference

Beinfield, Harriet, and Efrem Korngold. *Between Heaven and Earth.* New York: Random House, 1991.

Western Astrology and Feng Shui

Lin, Jami. *Earth Design.* Miami Shores, Fl.: Earth Design, 1995.

Index